How to Get a Date Worth Keeping

Resources by Henry Cloud

Changes That Heal
Changes That Heal Workbook
Changes That Heal audio

With John Townsend

Boundaries
Boundaries Workbook
Boundaries audio
Boundaries video curriculum
Boundaries Face to Face
Boundaries Face to Face audio
Boundaries in Dating
Boundaries in Dating Workbook
Boundaries in Dating audio
Boundaries in Dating curriculum
Boundaries in Marriage
Boundaries in Marriage Workbook
Boundaries in Marriage audio
Boundaries in Marriage curriculum
Boundaries with Kids
Boundaries with Kids Workbook
Boundaries with Kids audio
Boundaries with Kids curriculum
How People Grow
How People Grow Workbook
How People Grow audio
Making Small Groups Work
Making Small Groups Work audio
The Mom Factor
Raising Great Kids
Raising Great Kids for Parents of Preschoolers curriculum
Raising Great Kids Workbook for Parents of Preschoolers
Raising Great Kids Workbook for Parents of School-Age Children
Raising Great Kids Workbook for Parents of Teenagers
Raising Great Kids Audio Pages®
Safe People
Safe People Workbook
12 "Christian" Beliefs That Can Drive You Crazy

How to Get a Date Worth Keeping

Be Dating in Six Months or Your Money Back

Dr. Henry Cloud

GRAND RAPIDS, MICHIGAN 49530 USA

Some names have been changed in this book
to protect the privacy of the individuals involved.

ZONDERVAN™

How to Get a Date Worth Keeping
Copyright © 2005 by Henry Cloud

This title is also available as a Zondervan audio product.
Visit www.zondervan.com/audiopages for more information.

Requests for information should be addressed to:
Zondervan, *Grand Rapids, Michigan 49530*

Library of Congress Cataloging-in-Publication Data

Cloud, Henry
     How to get a date worth keeping / Henry Cloud—1st ed.
       p. cm.
     Includes bibliographical references and indexes.
     ISBN 0-310-26265-8
     1. Single people—Religious life. 2. Single people—Conduct of life. 3. Dating
(Social customs)—Religious aspects—Christianity. 4. Man-woman
relationships—Religious aspects—Christianity. I. Title.
BV4596.S5C59 2004
241'.6765—dc22

                                              2004024106

Published in association with Yates & Yates, LLP, Attorneys and Counselors, Suite 100, Literary Agent, Orange, CA.

Interior design by Michelle Espinoza

Printed in the United States of America

05 06 07 08 09 10 11 /❖ DCI/ 10 9 8 7 6 5 4 3 2 1

*To singles everywhere, with my hope that you can find
the experience of dating to be a great adventure—
fun, stretching, and fruitful!*

*And to the ones who have given me the privilege
of being your dating coach. You and your successes have been
an inspiration. Thanks for letting me be a part.*

Contents

Acknowledgments

Thanks to Sandy Vander Zicht, executive editor at Zondervan, who bugged me for a few years to write down the dating coaching program. Your persistence is what made this book a reality. Thanks, as always, for your commitment to the readers and to the fruit of their lives.

Thanks to Sealy Yates and Jeana Ledbetter of Yates and Yates. Without great agents, projects like this either would not happen, or they would not be all they could be. I appreciate your commitment to publishing and to my work over the years. You are good stewards of "message."

Thanks to the members of my community—you sustain me and give me so much. I thank God for you everyday.

Thanks to everyone at Cloud-Townsend Resources. You are a great family and team, and I love working with you. Your care for and commitment to the growth of others are a daily inspiration.

And special thanks to Lillie Nye Cashion for allowing me to write about you and Audie in this book. You dated with the courage and spirituality I wish all singles would bring to the task of changing their dating lives. I loved writing your story and recalling the great adventure you lived and I was privileged to watch. Way to go, guys!

Thanks also to singles pastors and leaders everywhere. You are shepherds over people in this process, and the work you do is invaluable. May God bless you!

A Heart to Heart from Your Coach

Pretend you are a contestant on the television game show *Jeopardy*. Contestants are given answers in various subject categories, and they need to come up with the question. Your category is "Single Life," and the answer is "Dating." What is the question?

You could come up with several winning questions:

- What's one of life's most exciting, energizing, and adventuresome activities?
- What's the one activity that can cause more angst and pain than anything else?
- What's the most debated and confusing topic?
- What activity can lead to more growth than almost any other?
- What's the activity for which singles get the least and often the worst training?
- What activity routinely has the most life-altering consequences of all others?
- What activity is one of the most important and weightiest, and yet about which the Bible is virtually silent?
- What activity do many married people long to do over again, the "right way this time"?

- What's the activity for which there are few rules, yet there is the need for many?

Ah, dating. How often we hear it longed for, hated, outlawed in some spiritual communities, put down, revered, and obsessed over. It remains the topic that takes up more space in a single person's heart, mind, and soul than anyone wants to admit. Why is that? Because it is both awesome in its potential for good and frightening in its potential for pain and destruction. And when it is stagnant, it is very depressing.

For these reasons some people spend a lot of time working on dating, and others run from it altogether. They give up when they have bad dating experiences, and some even advise people to avoid it completely.

In my own life and in my work with many singles over the years, I understand the dilemma. On the one hand, dating *can* be painful. It can cause setbacks and hurt. But on the other hand, dating can be a path to tremendous personal and spiritual growth, to great life experiences, and even to finding a marriage partner and building a new home.

So that brings up the question of this book: *How should a person date?* I began studying this question several years ago when singles asked me why they were not finding the dates they desired. They wondered what was wrong with them or with how they were going about dating. They wondered what was wrong with the men or the women "out there." They wondered where the good women and men were. Some even wondered if God cared.

When I ran into this problem over and over again, I formed some dating groups to figure out what the problem was, and then I developed a plan to solve the problem. In this book you will read about both the problem and a program designed to solve it.

This book will explain the things that cause both stagnant dating and unfruitful dating. Stagnant dating is when your dating life is virtually nonexistent or not as active as you desire. Unfruitful dating is when you are dating, but it is not going well; that is, you fall into recurrent destructive patterns, such as attracting the wrong types, not attracting the good ones, and having many other inappropriate or unhealthy patterns. We will explore both stale and unfruitful dating.

But understanding the problem is not enough. You also want to improve your dating life, so I will also tell you about a successful program I have taken many others through. The fun thing about this book is that it is not just a bunch of "theory"; it is a real-life program that others have found success with, all the way to marriage. It can provide lots of growth, healing, stretching, and *dates!*

If you are single and dating is not working as well as you would like, I feel for you. I've heard your predicament many times. This material comes out of real-life experiences, and my prayer is that you will find many, many dates worth keeping. Join me on this great adventure.

Part 1

What's the Problem?

Why Hasn't God Brought Me the Love of My Life?

The evening began routinely enough. The team producing my weekend seminar in Cincinnati and I were out to dinner. We discussed lighthearted things as we ordered our meal. It was more a moment to stop and catch our breath than to have life-altering discussions. Little did anyone know what was about to take place.

"I never thought I'd be doing what I'm doing now at this point in my life," Lillie said, innocently talking about her work.

"What do you mean?" I asked.

"Well, I always thought I would be married and have children by now."

Oh, I thought to myself. That makes sense. A lot of women feel that in their mid-thirties. I understood what she was saying, until she continued.

"But God hasn't chosen that for me."

My ears perked up. I wondered what she meant. While I believe that God leads us and guides us in life, I also wondered why she blamed her situation on God. Both the psychologist and the theologian in me bristled, wondering what responsibility she might be shirking regarding her undesired singleness. I knew her well enough to know she might have some issues contributing to her single state.

"What do you mean, 'God hasn't chosen that?'" I asked.

"Well, I believe God brings the man into your life you are to marry, and he hasn't brought that man to me yet," she replied. That was enough to get me going, but her next line really did it. "Or, he hasn't given me the feelings I would need for the men he has brought into my life."

"God hasn't 'given you the feelings?' What does that mean?"

"Well, God gives you the feelings for the person he wants you to marry, and that hasn't happened with any of the men I know."

"Whose feelings are they—yours or God's?"

"What do you mean?" she asked, sounding a little bugged.

"Well, it just sounds like you blame God for a lot. How do you know he hasn't brought *ten* great men into your life, but you have things inside of you that make you incapable of feeling what you would need to feel for them? How do you know your issues aren't getting in the way of recognizing and falling in love with a good man if he did come along? Why do you just assume this is God's fault?" I felt as though I was on a bit of a mission, defending God's honor.

"I disagree. God will bring the right man to me, and until then, I just need to wait."

"How is that going?"

"What do you mean?"

"Well, how long has it been since you went on a date?"

She hesitated, looking embarrassed. I didn't mean to put her on the spot; in fact, she had been so assertive in stating her case and so aggressive in coming after me when I challenged it that her sheepishness caught me off guard.

"Two years," she said.

"What?"

"It has been two years since I have been on a date," she confessed.

How could that be, I wondered. She was outgoing and attractive, a real people person of the highest order—traits that usually make dating come easily. Then it occurred to me. Her lack of dates had to be a combination of her sitting back and waiting for the man of her dreams to come and find her and some personal dynamics interfering with her desire to be married. I could think of no other reason someone who actually wanted to have a man in her life would be that stuck.

Then something changed in me. Up until that point, Lillie and I had been in a friendly debate. Everyone at the table had gotten caught up in the banter. But, when I saw the reality of the situation—an attractive young woman in the prime of her life, yet unhappy—I felt for her. I wanted to help. And if I were right, I knew I could. So, I issued a challenge:

"I will make you a deal, Lillie. I will be your dating coach. I guarantee that if you will do whatever I tell you, you will be dating in six months."

She looked at me, stunned. "What?"

"Just what I said. I'll be your dating coach, and if you will do whatever I say, I guarantee you'll be dating in six months. But there is a catch. I demand total obedience. You have to do everything I tell you, no questions asked. And I promise I will not ask you to do anything immoral, unethical, or illegal. But you have to do whatever I tell you."

Everyone at the table fell silent. I could see the others wondering whether or not *they* would subject themselves to such a mystery challenge. And I could see Lillie weighing the same thing. Did she really want to do such a crazy thing? Agree to conform to a totally unknown plan, just like that? I could also see that she was ticked at my challenging her "way" of thinking about dating. She wanted to accept the "bet" and prove me wrong. The latter attitude, I suspect, is what won out.

With the others hanging in suspense, she growled at me: "Fine. You're on."

I didn't really think she'd accept my challenge, but I was ready. I jumped right into it.

"Okay, here is your first assignment. For one month I want you to keep a log of all the new men you meet and email it to me at the end of every week. Send me the names so we can count how many new men come into your life and have a chance to ask you out."

"Are you joking?" she said. "I don't need an assignment for that. I can tell you right now. None."

"What do you mean, 'None'?" I asked.

"Exactly that. I never meet anyone new. Every day I go to the office and see the same six or eight people. Then I go home, eat dinner, and watch TV with my roommate. Then on Saturday, I run errands and hang out, and on Sunday I go to the same church and see the same people I always see. That is what happens every week. I never meet any new men to go out with."

"I don't care. I still want you to keep a log. And for the men to count, they have to fulfill three requirements. First, they have to be new men you've never met before. Second, they have to have enough of an interaction with you to want to ask you out. And, third, they have to have enough information to ask you out, such as your name or know how to find you. No pressure to have any dates right now. I just want to understand your situation. If the number is zero, that's fine. We can work with that. I just need to know what the picture really looks like."

She was not impressed with my first assignment. *How was calculating her misery going to get her a date?* she was probably wondering, thinking that this was going to be an easy challenge to win. But this assignment wasn't meant to help her get a date—yet. I was trying to get her to come out of denial and see the reality of her situation.

For two years her dating life had been stagnant, and she was denying that reality with a philosophy that if you do nothing, God will somehow step in and provide a man. That way of thinking, which I knew was nowhere in the Bible, kept her from seeing she was very, very stuck. My goal was to get her to see the reality of her situation and to get very discouraged. I wanted her to see that what she was doing was not working and that it had been that way for a long time. I wanted that realization to sink in and bother her. My trying to convince her that she was wrong was not going to work. She was too sure she was right. I wanted her to realize the reality of her dating life for herself. Just as balancing a checkbook can wake one up to one's lack of money, keeping a log would awaken Lillie to her lack of dates.

I had many other assignments lurking in the back of my mind to give her. And after she completed this first one, I gave them to her one by one. She obeyed, fully. I have to hand it to her: She stuck with the "program."

Here is the result: In five months, she was in a significant dating relationship. So, I won the bet. But it didn't end there. Just a few months ago, I officiated at her wedding to a wonderful man.

When I talked to her the other day, she laughed about how it had all happened. "Being married is so cool," she said. And then she stopped herself and quickly added, "But it is only cool if you are with the right person."

I was so happy for her. She got her dream, and she got it with a good person. That to me was the full victory: not just to be dating—usually an easily achievable goal—but to be dating a *good* person, the kind worth keeping.

That is the goal of this book. I not only want you to have a wonderful dating life, but I also want those dates to be with good people: "the kind worth keeping."

In this book I will give you a strategy to get your dating life moving in that direction: more dates, and more dates with good people. I will take you through the program I took Lillie through and give you some added tips as well. And I believe that if you are ready to follow my advice, you too can find a date worth keeping. Are you ready? I hope so.

But, to find out, let's take a gut check first.

Gut Check

Before you read any further in this book, I want to be honest with you. In working with many singles who want to improve their dating lives, I have found three common reactions to my advice. My hunch is that you will find yourself having one of these three as well:

1. You may get angry.

This is what Lillie did, at first. She got mad at me for a couple of reasons. First, I was challenging her way of thinking about a very important area of her life, and she became defensive. This is understandable. Often when someone challenges our views on issues important to our hearts, it can provoke anxiety. We want to fight off that challenge to views that give us a sense of security.

Second, she became angry because I was implying that she was at least partly responsible for her dateless situation. I was saying that it was not just God's fault for not bringing a man into her life. Now remember, I do believe God directs us and brings people into our lives—not just in dating, but in every area of life. As the psalmist says:

The LORD is my shepherd, I shall not be in want.
He makes me lie down in green pastures,
he leads me beside quiet waters,
he restores my soul.

(Ps. 23:1–3a)

God guides and provides, but he also requires us to do our part.

I will talk about this more later, but let me just say here that if you think you have no responsibility in your life for getting the things you want, I may make you mad because I am going to tell you that you do. So, if being held accountable for your dating life is going to bug you, this book is going to bug you.

2. You may get discouraged.

Some people, when encouraged to take ownership for an area of life, quickly blame themselves in a critical way. They say things like, "See, I really *am* a loser. It's all my fault I'm like this. I can never do anything right. My parents told me I was a loser, and they were right. I deserve what I'm getting."

If you respond this way, please hear that I'm not blaming you for things not going well. First of all, even though I told Lillie she shared responsibility for her situation, I was not saying that life does not deal us some tough hands. Circumstances we can't control are forced upon us. Sometimes those influence dating. They are not your fault.

If things have happened to you that have made dating difficult, don't blame yourself. If you have been abused, or if you are depressed, lonely, shy, and afraid of people, don't blame yourself; get help. That is what I mean by "ownership"—to put your arms around your issues, get help, and grow.

Also, there may be some things you can do but you've been ignoring. When you hear me tell you to do those things, I'm not condemning you for not doing them. I'm coaching you and nudging you to take some steps and get moving.

3. You may take ownership and become empowered.

This is how I hope you will respond. There *are* things you can do. In fact, you are *supposed* to be a writer and director of your life as well as an actor. Don't just act in the play of your life, but write the script as well. You don't have to stay stuck. If you are ready to take a hard look at your life and change it, with God's help, I believe you can. This is the response I'm looking for from you. If you put into practice the things we are talking about, you can change your dating life.

I want you to hear what I am saying as motivating, and then get with the program.

So, if you get angry, talk to someone to see why a book suggesting that you can do something to help yourself bugs you. If you get discouraged, get some help for your self-criticism. Beating yourself up will not help you and can even be dangerous to your well-being.

But, if you're ready to get unstuck, don't just sit there. Get motivated. I have seen these strategies bring successful dating to many people. Let's grab your dating life by the horns and get moving. It's time to get a date worth keeping.

3

Where I Am Coming From

||||||||||||||||||||||||||||||

Why should you trust what I say in this book? Fair question. Let me take a few minutes to explain where I'm coming from, what I think about dating, and how it can change your life.

My interest in helping people who were stuck in dating began a decade ago. Every year I did several week-long training sessions for an organization that had a lot of single people in its leadership. We held the training at a resort, and the week was structured to give us time to interact and to have down time. This gave me the chance to get to know many of the singles in more depth.

I began to notice a pattern. About the third night of every conference, after dinner, in the "hang out" time, a group of single women would approach me, saying, "We have a question. Can we talk to you?"

We would find a place to sit and talk. Amazingly, each group would virtually look alike, sound alike, and say the same thing: "Why don't we have any dates?" These attractive, interesting, educated, outgoing single women all wondered the same thing. Why were they stuck? Why were they not realizing what they desired in this important area of life?

As they approached symbolic milestones, such as turning thirty or forty, the question became even more bothersome. Passing these milestones, or having friends who dated regularly or were getting engaged and married, underscored their own dissatisfaction. They weren't clinically depressed about it; they were just bummed about their lack of dates, and they wondered if there was an answer to their question.

Interested, I decided to study the problem with them, and with others, including men. I became a sleuth. I volunteered to become a dating coach to figure out this problem. I formed dating groups to find out more. As I traveled around speaking at seminars and to various groups, a lot of singles—men and women—voiced the same complaints. The pervasiveness of this issue surprised me.

At first I was tempted to buy into the single men and women's summation of the problem:

- "There are just no good men out there. They are already taken."
- "I live somewhere where there is no one to date."
- "There are not enough women 'out there.'"
- "The attractive ones don't have values, and the spiritual ones are boring."

They made the problem sound circumstantial. I would hear these explanations over and over again. Sometimes there was a grain of truth to these complaints. Sometimes they did live in an area in which the ratio of single men to single women was against them. They almost lured me into thinking we needed to work on how to find some eligible men and women to solve their dilemma.

The Real Truth

But then I remembered what I have come to believe over and over again. *Our lives are not just about the "outside" circumstances.* There is usually more to it than that. If our career is not working, it is not only because the economy is in a tough place, although that can certainly be a factor. If we are overweight, it is not only because we are under a lot of stress. If we are broke, it is not only because we don't make enough money. Outside factors in life, such as a tough economy, a stressful marriage, or a minimum-wage job, influence us, to be sure. I would have to be an idiot not to acknowledge that. But it is about us as well. *We participate* in our external circumstances. We may not cause them, but we can control how we respond to them.

If, for example, you live in a small town and you know every unmarried person there, you did not cause that town to have so few eligible men or women. But you can choose what you will do with that fact. Will you stay there? Will you travel to a nearby town and build a community there? Will you move? Will you do nothing? Will you join a dating service that can match you with people from nearby areas? Will you blame God? All of these are possible responses to the same outside circumstance.

Philosophers over the years have referred to this responsibility for our own life as "existential responsibility." We do not cause our existence, but we *participate* in it, and we are responsible for dealing with it and, as a result, have a hand in creating it and changing it.

Active Dating

So, first, as a dating coach, my way of thinking about this problem was, "Okay, so there are no eligible women and men in your town, church, organization, or life. What are you going to do with that reality? How are you going to respond to it? You did not cause it, but it is in your life, so it is your responsibility to respond to it. If it really is a numbers problem, why aren't you doing something about it?"

Second, as a psychologist, I believe that our own internal psychological dynamics play a part in our external situations. Sometimes "who we are" creates some of the situations in which we find ourselves. What inner dynamics of these single people were contributing to their "stuckness"? How were these people, even unconsciously, contributing to their problem? There was something here worth exploring.

Third, and most important to me as a Christian, I believe strongly in spiritual dynamics. God has set up the universe in certain ways, and those ways are dependable. Spiritual principles say we share responsibility in making our lives better. I could think of several passages from the Bible that said that, such as this passage from the apostle Paul's letter to the Philippians:

> *Therefore, my dear friends, as you have always obeyed —not only in my presence, but now much more in my absence*—continue to work out your salvation with fear and trembling, *for it is God who works in you to will and to act according to his good purpose.*
>
> (Phil. 2:12–13, emphasis mine)

Salvation in this verse means deliverance, healing, or rescuing. In other words, God will help and do his part, but these women and men had to get busy and do their part, as they did in other areas of their lives.

Many people have been taught to view dating similarly to the way Lillie did: "God will bring the person to you. Just wait." And they think this approach is spiritual. But, in reality, it negates the dual track of the Bible that teaches God will guide the way, but we have to actively walk in that way and fight the battles.

One woman called our radio show angry with me because I believed in active dating. She accused me of "bad teaching" and of being "out of step with the Bible." She said that the Bible teaches people should sit back and wait on God.

"So, how far would you take that thinking?" I asked. "Are you saying that you are not supposed to do *anything* in this area of your life?"

"Yes. That's right. I trust God enough to just bring a husband to me."

"So how far do you take that?" I asked again. "Do you think you don't have to go out at all? Do you think God will just bring a man to your door one day if you do nothing?"

"Absolutely. I believe God can bring him to my door. I trust him that much."

"So, how is it working? How long have you been doing this?"

"For many years," she said resolutely, as though to prove her point. I felt as though she proved mine. Just waiting for her husband to show up at her door, she had no dates. So, I told her what I thought was a spiritual reality.

"Lady," I said, "if you don't want to marry the FedEx man or a Jehovah's Witness, you had better go outside!"

You get my point. The Bible teaches that God provides, even for the birds of the air (Matt. 6:25–34), but the birds have to leave the nest and fly around to find the mosquitoes or the seeds God provides! *There is some activity required on their part.*

This caller tried to argue that God brought Rebecca to Isaac. Very true, but what she neglected to acknowledge was that Abraham sent out a search team to find his son a wife (Gen. 24:1–11). God was doing his part, but so was Abraham. He was *active*, and God was faithful. Just as the parable of the talents teaches, it is possible to bury one's life in the ground and not invest oneself by getting active and taking risks. And the result is that years go by, and there is no gain. God promises to be faithful, but he also tells us to get moving.

For some reason, people are taught that in every area of life, except dating, they are to be diligent and responsible. If God calls you to be an engineer, for example, you go to college, study hard, get a degree, seek a job, and go on interviews *to fulfill this purpose.* If you want to be in a church, you don't just hope one will find you. You visit a number of churches, check them out, and see how they fit with what you need and what you feel God is leading you to become. If you want to build a community of friends, you don't just sit at home. You seek them where they can be found, and you reach out and meet them. You are active, and you achieve your desire.

As I listened to these women, I felt there was more to the story than just a "numbers" problem of not "finding enough good men." Deeper spiritual and psychological issues were at work. I thought this also because I had already worked with many singles who had been stuck and had gotten unstuck as they had worked through certain dynamics. Without getting ahead of ourselves, have you ever wondered why two equally attractive and interesting women or men can be sitting at a party, and someone sees them and is instantly drawn to one and not the other? Of course you have. You have done that yourself.

That is an example of how people can attract or not attract others and not even know it, and that ability to attract others comes from things going on *inside* of them. Later on we'll talk about why this happens.

In addition, I often hear this question: "Why do the ones I'm not interested in always like me and the ones I like are not attracted to me?" Trust me, this has a lot to do with the internal issues we will talk about in this book—issues you can take control of and change.

Dating, like the rest of life, is not just about a "bad market." It is not primarily about numbers and the availability of eligible men and women of the opposite sex. It is much more about *your* availability and eligibility. This is my view, and I'm sticking to it. My mission in this book is to help you become healthy and available in this arena of your life, so you will be able to not only find a date but find one worth keeping. I truly believe as you make certain changes inside, the outside world of your dating life will change as well.

So, let me sum up where I'm coming from:

- Dating, like the rest of life, is subject to circumstances outside of your control. To a certain extent, you may have a numbers problem. Finding good people of the opposite sex is a problem to be solved.
- Dating, like the rest of life, is also subject to things that have happened to you and that are not your fault. If you have been hurt and are afraid of risk, you did not cause that. Do not get down on yourself.
- Dating, like the rest of life, is also subject to the reality that even the things that you did not cause are still your

responsibility to deal with. The Bible teaches—and philosophy, psychology, and experience all validate it—that it is going to take some activity on your part to deal with the numbers issues, your trust issues, your fear factors, or whatever other realities you might have encountered. This part of life is your responsibility, just like every other area.

- Dating, like the rest of life, is also an expression of our own personal makeup. It is very possible that the reason this area of your life is not working for you has something to do with unresolved issues in your own life. As you begin to grow in those areas, which we will explore, your dating will be affected.

- Dating, like the rest of life, is subject to the created order of God's design. He gives us seeds and land. We have to sow the seeds and work the soil of our lives to be fruitful. In other words, for dating to work, you have to be active. In addition, just as God does in other areas of life, God will lead you and help you along the way. God does his part, and you do yours. Remember, God secured the promised land, but the Israelites had to make the journey, fight the battles, and grow to possess it.

- Dating, like the rest of life, has certain risks. If you are too hurt right now to risk dating, this may not be the time for you to do the kinds of things I will suggest in this book. If you are at risk for serious depression or other clinical issues, you should see a good professional and work on those first. If you are an alcoholic, you should not go to a bar. If you are a sex addict, or impulsive, and are in danger of high-risk behavior in this realm, you should not be out there doing the kinds of things I will suggest. You should be in recovery and get well first.

- Dating, like the rest of life, can be extremely discouraging. Especially in our culture and society, forces are in play that can work against you. I was single well into my adult life, so I understand your difficulties not only from being a dating "coach," but also from having been out there in the fray myself. It can be fun, but it can be discouraging and heart-breaking as well. So, as we go forward, don't just think that this is "one more married person who doesn't understand." I do understand how hard it can be, but I also know it can be made better.

Dating is not only a wonderful time of life, but also a context for enormous spiritual and personal growth. You learn so much about yourself, others, God, love, spirituality, and life through dating. Done well, it can be fulfilling in and of itself. Done well, it can be one of the most fun and rewarding aspects of your life. Done well, it can lead to a good marriage.

I don't know what your particular goal is in reading this book, but mine is to guide you through the steps that will make a real difference in your dating life so that you say goodbye to dating doldrums and hello to a great adventure.

If we accomplish that together, then I am sure another goal will be accomplished as well: You will have grown as a person. The two goals, dating successfully and growing personally, will go together. The spiritual and personal growth you will experience is half the fun. You will be stretched, but it will be an adventure, and the experience will be well worth the effort.

As Lillie told me the other day, "I never imagined how much fun it could be with the right person." I pray that for you too.

4

Dating Is Not about Marriage

"You just said that we ought to date a lot of people to learn and grow and all that stuff, but I really disagree," said a woman seated in the first row at one of my seminars. "I don't have time for that."

"What do you mean, 'You don't have time for that?'" I could tell the questioner was young and energetic. What could she mean that she didn't have time for dating? Usually you hear that from someone worried about his or her age in some way, such as a man worrying about putting down roots or a woman worrying about her biological clock. Maybe that is what she meant, I thought.

"I don't have time to waste on dating someone whom I couldn't see myself marrying. If he doesn't have the potential for a serious relationship that could lead to marriage, I don't want to go out with him."

"What's your hurry?"

"Well, I'm forty-two, I've been married once before, and I want to be married again. I don't have time to waste."

"I don't get it. You are only forty-two. It's not like your life is over. What's your hurry?"

"Well, I just don't have time for all this dating. I only want to go out with someone I could marry. Isn't that the purpose of dating? To find a mate?"

"NO! NO! NO!" I said, literally jumping up and down on the stage. If I could have screamed louder without breaking the microphone, I would have. "That is not the sole purpose of dating! Haven't you heard anything I've said?"

"Well, I just couldn't believe you were really serious about dating just for dating. I date to find a *mate*."

I did not know any of the facts of her life. But I did know a lot from what she was saying. She was in a hurry, and on the hunt. That was easy enough to see. And that always means something. But past that, she was showing something else. It sounded like she thought she knew what she wanted and needed. I seriously doubted that.

"So, tell me about the last ten years," I said, picking a number out of the air. I wondered how her dating plan of action was going.

"Bad marriage and divorce," she said.

This answer did not tell me a lot about her dating, so I pressed her. "How long have you been divorced?"

"It is not final yet. We ended it two weeks ago."

The crowd gasped.

"*What*? Your divorce is not final, and you are already 'in a hurry?'" I could hardly believe my ears, although I should have. I have seen this countless times. "So what you are telling me is this. The last time you chose someone, it ended in disaster. And you have chosen no one since him, right?" With only two weeks on the market, I assumed she had not been in another relationship.

"Right."

"So you have made one choice for a mate, and it was a bad choice. Isn't it obvious that your 'people picker' is broken? Now, with no further experience dating, you think you are ready to make *another* lifetime commitment with the same people picker you used to pick the last one. No, no, no! You are not ready to date to find a mate. You obviously do not know what you need, what is good and what is not good, and what your unhealthy patterns are. You are 0 for 1.

"The last thing you need is to date to find a mate. You need more than anyone to go out with many different kinds of men for a number of reasons. There is no way you are ready to think that you know what you need or what is good for you. The last ten years should have proven that to you. Make a commitment to not make a commitment. That is what you need to do. Go into divorce recovery. Get healing. Get therapy. But, *please* do not go out looking for another mate. That is the last thing you need."

This is one of the biggest problems I've encountered in my work with singles and dating. Do not let the questioner's recent divorce confuse the issue; I'm not talking about the need to avoid a rebound. The real issue here is what is the purpose of dating. One of the first steps people need is to be cured of the thinking that the purpose of dating is to find a marriage partner. This is often a result, obviously. But here is what I'm trying to say:

Dating is as much about learning what you need and want, and how you need to grow and change, as it is about finding the "right" person.

Look at it this way. Tiger Woods grew up with the goal of winning more major golf tournaments than anyone in history. He wanted to win more U.S. Opens, Masters, PGAs, and British Opens than Jack Nicklaus did. What if Tiger had said early on, "I will not play in any other tournament than the U.S. Open." Ridiculous. What if any other athlete said, "I will only play in the Super Bowl, or the World Series." That's crazy. Or what if a medical student said, "I will only take the ultimate job in my life's career? I will not work at anything less than that." I would not want to go to that surgeon.

Some people approach dating like that. They think they know what they need, what they want, or who they need to be. We will see specific reasons why this is not true in upcoming chapters, but for now I want you to join me in taking a hard look at your dating philosophy. If you have seen it as only a search for the love of your life, then I want you to make some shifts in your thinking. I want you to see dating in a very, very different way.

1. See dating as a wonderful time to find out about other people and what they are like.

The recently divorced woman at my seminar needed to date a lot of men to find out how "off" she was in her ability to see what is good and to pick a good man. Without dating for the sake of learning, she would not do that. She would just jump into another relationship where she felt "in love."

You might have no clue what is "out there" in the world of the opposite sex. I sent one young man out on a date with someone I knew he would not be attracted to. He was looking for a certain type, and she would not normally have been "on his list." Afterward, he told me he had the best four hours talking to her about her spiritual life; he had never experienced that depth with a woman before. This interaction with a deeply spiritual woman who was not his "type" taught him something. He would never have known that he could have that kind of connection if he had seen dating as only "finding a mate," because she would not have been one he thought he could marry. He would never have gone out on a date with her.

This experience has affected what he is looking for, and it has also caused him to avoid some shallow women. He found something he really needs in a serious relationship from just dating nonseriously. What he is attracted to changed as a result. He is now turned off by spiritual shallowness, and he looks for spiritual depth.

Another woman told me that going out on dates just to date taught her that a man could listen to her. She had been drawn to a certain type of self-centered man. When she followed this strategy of dating to learn, she discovered that more was available than what she had settled for and that not all men were like those she had seen. She learned about different kinds of men from "just dating."

Dating is an opportunity to meet and get to know many different kinds of people. Expect dating to expand your view of what is good and what you find attractive in the opposite sex. Stop evaluating women and men by some criteria they have to pass or fail, and just observe, notice, and get to know them instead. You will find valuable things you may never have seen before.

2. See dating as a wonderful time to find out about yourself and how you need to change.

When you are dating to learn, you can monitor your feelings, reactions, and character as you meet different kinds of people. One woman I know was always drawn to passive men who were kind; however, her dating experiences with these men were frustrating. She realized that her tastes in men were coming out of a wounded place inside of her: Her father had been overly aggressive, and she was afraid of strong men. She needed to get to a place where a stronger man would not feel like her aggressive father and push her buttons. She did this by dating stronger men and making the changes inside to where she could actually like a man with a sense of backbone instead of going for a wimp to feel safe.

As you date for fun, you will be in many different situations that will give you feedback on yourself that you need to know. How do you respond with a certain kind of person? Why? Are you threatened by a certain kind of person? Why? Do you go brain dead with a certain kind of person? Why? Do you feel more "alive" or "dead" with a certain kind of person? Why? Those are good things to find out. As you figure out who you are in relation to others, you will be more prepared to pick someone good.

3. See dating as an end in and of itself.

How do you know if marriage is in the cards for you, and, if it is, how do you know when it will happen? I, for one, did not marry until well into my thirties. I loved my dating years. They were a lot of fun, and I had wonderful experiences getting to know some really good women.

Dating is an activity where you do fun, meaningful things with interesting people. This is a great goal in and of itself. If you are not having fun dating, then something is wrong. You might be judging each person you go out with by whether or not he or she is "marriage material." If you decide he or she is not, then you deem the date of no value.

What's wrong? Didn't you enjoy the movie? Or the conversation? Or the food? Come on, *have a good time!* Don't spoil a meaningful experience just because you did not find the love of your life. Tiger Woods enjoys not only the U.S. Open, but also a round of golf on Tuesday afternoon with his friends.

Date to have fun. Date to learn. Date to experience things. If you are only dating to marry, you are not experiencing life, and you are missing out on knowing a lot of good people along the way.

4. See dating in a way that takes the pressure off.

One woman I worked with was so afraid of rejection she sabotaged her dating life. She worried so much about whether or not a guy was going to like her that she could not enjoy the date. As a result, she was always less than herself, and the guy never got to see who she really was. She actually experienced much more rejection because the guys she dated never really saw all she had to offer.

I advised her to look at a date as an activity to get to know someone and spend some time doing something fun, with no pressure. She stopped looking for a potential mate or serious relationship, and it all changed. She finally learned how to be who she really was with a man. Her dating increased, her anxiety went down, and she started taking baby steps down the path to finding what she wanted.

If every date is the Super Bowl, you will put too much pressure on yourself to win. Just enjoy the game!

5. See dating as an opportunity to love and serve others.

Just as you learn as you date, so do the people you go out with. When you treat your dates as you would want them to treat you and show them what a good man or woman is like, you have served them. When you have relationships with people, you leave a wake behind, similar to the backwash a boat leaves behind. When you date, leave a wake where the person is better off for having known you.

Dating is a give and take. If you only see it as "taking," you are not getting it. See dating as a time to show others what being treated well looks like; then you help them see what is good in life, and you love and serve them. You never know where someone has come from—to be treated well might turn them around for good. "Do unto others as you would have them do unto you." Help them to see what "good" is, and show them God's design for good relationship. All of life, including dating, should be a place where you are learning to love others better.

6. See dating as an opportunity to grow in skills.

Dating is a place to practice how to relate to other people. If you know you need to be more direct, for example, practice with your dates. If you need to learn how to open up and talk about yourself, your feelings, and your wants, practice it in dating. If you need to learn how to confront others and deal with conflict, practice it in dating. Or maybe you need to learn how to deny yourself, listen to others, or be less self-centered. Dating is a place where you can bring all the parts of you that need spiritual growth.

If you never learn basic relationship skills *before* that special someone comes along, you are in trouble. You will not be able to do what you need to do in the relationship that matters most, and you may ruin it. In addition, if you don't learn mature relational skills, you will probably fall in love out of your dysfunction. So, use low-risk dating as a place to practice being a more mature person.

7. Perhaps promise yourself that you will make no serious commitment for a certain length of time.

Make a commitment to try this approach for a certain period of time. I recently made a friend promise me that he would not get into an exclusive dating relationship for six months. Even if he found a woman he really liked, he had to stay unattached, or nonexclusive, for six months. I gave him this assignment because I knew he did not know what he needed and wanted, and I wanted him to grow in self-knowledge.

Interestingly enough, he did meet a woman with whom he wanted to get serious, but he kept his commitment to see other women as well. This helped him to evaluate the one he really liked. It looks like he might commit to her. That is great, but if he does, he will be coming from a much more complete place than he would have if he had not dated others.

Changing your goal and expectations of dating from looking for a mate to learning and experiencing will do wonderful things for you. You are probably not ready to marry if you have always demanded that dating was for serious relationships only. Begin by taking the following pledge:

> **I will date as an end in and of itself. I will no longer see dating as a place only to find a mate, but as a place to learn, grow, experience, and serve other people. It is my new laboratory of learning, growth, and experience.**

That is the first step in this program. See dating as a place not to find a mate but to learn and have fun.

Part 2

The Program

5

Keep a Log

Now it's time to get moving. But don't worry. I'm not going to send you out on a scary assignment right away. Instead, I want you to study the problem. I want you to observe yourself. In the same way Solomon said, "What a shame, what folly, to give advice before listening to the facts" (Prov. 18:13, NLT), I don't want you to try to fix your dating problems before you even know what they are. I want you to really know your dating problem, look it squarely in the eye, and put your arms around it.

There are two basic dating problems: no dates, or the wrong dates. In this book we are going to address the causes of both and do some things to fix them. But, first, you need to do exactly the assignment I gave to Lillie on the first night.

Step One: Log the Number of Eligibles You Meet Each Week

Keep a log for two weeks or up to a month and review it with your teammates each week. (See chapter 11, "Get Your Team Together," on how to create a team.) This log is easy to keep. It only has two pieces of information on it. First is the number of eligibles you meet this week who fulfill these three requirements:

1. They are new to you. (This doesn't mean that you have never seen them before. You may have seen them or even been introduced, but there was no real interaction between you.)
2. They have enough of an interaction with you to want to go out with you.
3. You have enough information about each other to follow through on that desire.

If you think about it, this is the formula for a date:

New people + interest + ability to follow through = a date

If you take any one ingredient out of the equation, no new date is going to happen. You can meet someone but have no telephone number or way to find her again, and she is lost forever. You can see someone, observe him, and be interested, but if he doesn't talk to you or have some way to get interested, nothing will happen. These three ingredients are essential.

Step Two: Log the Reason for the Number

At the end of the time, ask yourself why the number is what it is. Good or bad, why is that the number? This is the second piece of information for your log. Let's look at a few examples.

Remember what Lillie told me when I gave her the assignment? She said the answer would be zero. Actually, her guess turned out to be fairly accurate. (She did go to a convention soon after I gave her the assignment, which made one week's numbers go artificially high.) After she kept the log, it made total sense why she was not dating. She went to work every weekday, saw the same small group of people, went home, ate dinner with her roommate, and watched TV till bedtime. That was just about every day. On Saturday she might go out, but usually alone or with friends she had known for a long time. On Sunday she went to church with the same group of people she had known forever.

Lillie had an obvious numbers problem. She was basically depending on FedEx. If someone did not send her a package that got delivered by the man God had chosen for her, not much was going to happen. She was not sowing and thus she was not reaping. Plain and simple. We will talk later about the reasons behind her passive approach, but for now, I want you to realize what she realized. There is a reason that the number is whatever it is. After keeping a log, she realized she had retreated into a routine life that did not include new dating prospects. That was reality. She was going to have to do something about that.

But, let's look at another scenario—one that she encountered later. Let's say you are not as reclusive as Lillie and you actually do go to places where you have the opportunity to meet new people, but you come home with no new names to add to your log. Why? That is a question I want you to answer.

Perhaps you went to your company's convention, at which there was a big opening night party. There were new people there you had never met before. You saw three that were attractive or interesting to you but you did not meet them, or if you met them you did not fulfill requirement number two and interact with them enough to hook their interest. So, you came home with zero names for your log. Why didn't you talk to them? Why didn't you introduce yourself? Why didn't you go up to the buffet line and ask, "Did you have the fish?" and "How was it?" Or why didn't you ask the person you know who was talking to the three new people to introduce you?

Once you consider the reason why your number is what it is, you have a better idea of what you need to work on to get the numbers where you want them to be. To give you an idea of what you might find once you start keeping a log, here are a few examples of self-defeating patterns that people I've coached discovered in looking at their behavior for each of the three log requirements.

No New Eligibles

Reasons for not meeting requirement one: "They are new to you."

- You turn down invitations to go places because you don't ever think it will be worth it.

- You prejudge the kinds of people you will meet there and don't think they will be eligibles.
- You are not invited anywhere, so you do nothing to create new activities or places to go or other ways that you might meet someone.
- The places you get invited to do not fit into your "narrow box of acceptable options." For example, you turn down a friend from work who invites you to go out after work to a respectable establishment where normal people gather to talk and mingle.
- You have no confidence in the taste of the people who offer to introduce you to someone.
- You are aware of dating services or other proven methods of meeting people, but have a stigma against them without trying them out.

No Interaction

Reasons for not meeting requirement two: "They have enough interaction with you to want to go out with you."

- "That is too forward. I could never do that."
- "I am too shy. It's too scary to walk up to someone and begin a conversation."
- "They will think I am hitting on them."
- "I look fat."
- "I'm not handsome."
- "I can't do that. I don't know anything about them. What if they don't share my same values?"
- "What if they don't like me? I might get rejected."

No Contact Information

Reasons for not meeting requirement three: "You have enough information about each other to follow through."

- You have a great conversation with someone and then realize you have to go and just say good bye. There was no, "I have really enjoyed chatting. Give me your email address and let's go for coffee sometime."

- You interact with someone, and you know that a mutual person has the way to connect the two of you but you are too afraid to ask.
- You interact with someone and may not know how to get connected, and you do not look for how to do so. (See the first example in chapter 22, "Where Is the Testosterone?")

It really doesn't matter why you are not meeting new people, record it. It is the reason. Period. No excuses and no explaining it away. The one thing I want you to see at this point is that reality is reality. What is going on in your life is going on. You must own that if anything is going to change.

The purpose of logging eligibles and examining the reasons for the weekly numbers total is to understand the extent of the problem and the pattern of how it happens. On the one hand, you may discover you are sitting on a wealth of new prospects and are not being active enough to get connected. On the other hand, you might be in a desert without any water in view. Or, you may have a lot of possibilities, but you are allowing fears or beliefs to get in the way. For whatever reason, something is driving the failure and you need to know what it is in order to address it later. But for now, just identify what it is. This is an important step.

Step Three: Own the Reason for the Numbers and Play the Movie

In my book *Nine Things You Simply Must Do*, I talk about a principle called "Play the Movie." What I mean by this is that whatever you are doing in any situation is only a scene in a bigger movie. For example, let's say Lillie's schedule was the way it was: She was not meeting anyone, and she was doing nothing to change that week after week. If she doesn't see that each week is a scene in a larger movie, it would be easy for her to let this continue to happen without realizing that she is on her way to two years without a date.

Each day, if you never realize that your movie is headed somewhere, it is possible for you to let years go by and not make any changes because you only think about that day or that week. You say to yourself on any given Saturday night, "Oh, I have no plans tonight. I wonder what I will do." Then you just deal with that night without seeing the larger picture of the story you are writing.

But, if you play the movie all the way to the end, you realize that if you make no changes to the way you are living your life in this area, *next Saturday you will not have a date. And the next one you will not have a date. And the next one you will not have a date.* And you will not have a date for the Christmas party. And you will be watching a DVD alone on New Year's Eve. And you will be going out with your friends on Valentine's Day. The principle is this: If you continue to do what you are doing, play that out into the future and see if you like the way your life looks five years from now.

When Lillie did that, she got depressed.

This is one of the most powerful things the Bible tells us to do: Look at our current behavior and where it is going to lead, and see if you like the end result. When you don't like what you see, something good happens. You get bummed, and you repent. You change your mind. You see the extent of the problem. In fact, the definition of repentance is to "get it." When you "get it," you tend to change. It hits home.

I want you to get a real picture of your life of dating, the way you are going about it, the results it's bringing you, and what your future will look like if you do not do something different. Remember the old saying, "To continue to do the same thing expecting different results is the definition of crazy." Understand what you are doing. If you don't make some changes, the result will be the same.

Once you do that, you will be more motivated to make the changes I'm going to ask you to make.

6

If You Say, "There Are No Good Prospects," You Don't Get It

As I traveled around the country, I kept hearing from good, interesting, spiritual, desirable people: "Why don't we have dates?" "Where are the good ones?" "There just aren't any good ones out there." It was a little bizarre, if you think about it.

When I talked with a group of women, they would complain that there were no good, spiritual men "out there." They would have me believing that the world was either a convent with no men anywhere, or a men's penitentiary, with lots of men, but none you would want to take home for fear of what they might do to you. Or more to the point, a lot of men they would *like* to take home, but none they would want to *build* a home with. Many of them seemed to be drawn to men they knew were not good for them, and at the same time they knew that these "players" were not the ones who shared their spiritual values.

When I talked with a group of guys, I would hear *exactly* the same thing: There are no attractive, spiritual women "out there." Many of them had a romantic ideal image they would be drawn to, but the women who fit that image they would find vacuous over time. At the same time, they would often have platonic friendships with quality, spiritual women, but not be attracted to them.

The question that loomed in my mind is obvious: "Why aren't these two groups finding each other? They are saying exactly the same things." It weighed on me, and I wondered how to help them.

Then my moment of enlightenment came. At a seminar in Southern California, I talked about picking people of character and spiritual values to date. When we got to the question-and-answer time, a woman raised her hand and said, "You talk about dating lots of people to learn what kind of person you need and the importance of finding ones with spiritual values. Well, that's impossible in Southern California. People here are just too independent and into themselves. They are also transient. They have no roots. They are all 'new,' and really flighty. It would be a lot easier to find the kind of person you are talking about in the Midwest."

I almost could not contain myself. I wanted to yell at her.

The day before, I had been speaking in the Midwest, and a woman from the audience had said, "It is hard to find good men here. Most of the ones around here are not really into spiritual things, and those who are have lived here for a long time and are not available. It would be easier in a place like California, where there are more new people."

So, the West Coast woman who lived in a greater metropolitan area of over twenty million people said all the good men were in the Midwest. And the Midwest woman said they were all on the West Coast. Anyone see a problem?

I knew men and women on the West Coast who were finding good dates, and I coached others in the Midwest who were finding them as well. The woman's comment reinforced something I already knew:

Those who blame external circumstances for their situation do not find what they want. Those who work on themselves, take responsibility for dealing with their circumstances, and then take action, have success.

I wanted to scream, "Stop seeing the problem as only on the outside and begin to work on yourself."

Get Converted

I want to convert you to a way of thinking that might seem crazy to you, but which will improve your dating life. The book of Proverbs expresses it well:

> *Above all else, guard your heart,*
> *for it is the wellspring of life.*
> *(Prov. 4:23)*

What this proverb means is that our external life comes out of our internal life. In other words, the outside comes from the inside. The word *wellspring* is sometimes translated to mean the issues that spring forth into one's life from the heart. What does that have to do with dating? The "issues" in your dating life may have something to do with your "heart," or your internal life.

What are the "issues" in one's dating life? They could be anything from "I never meet anyone new," to "I am getting asked out by more people than I can work into my schedule!" The first issue comes out of one's inner world. Remember the woman from the previous chapter who never met anyone new because she was too afraid to introduce herself to new people? Her fear is an internal issue. Or the guy who reports that a woman avoids him after he asks her out? Something is causing that to happen.

The second "issue," having too many dates, is a good one to have. And it also comes from one's inner world, but it is an inner world of confidence, a heart that reaches out to people and gives off messages of openness and invitation. It is an attitude of taking risks and joining a good dating service or networking well, and an openness to many different kinds of people, among a lot of other things, as we will see.

In either example, good or bad, the outside world is coming from the inside world. The person's attitudes, beliefs, feelings, and fears are coming to fruition. Why do some people step out, develop a talent, believe in themselves, invest that talent, fail miserably, get up again, and finally succeed and build a career? Why do others sit on that talent or that desire, and never express it? What is the difference?

It is not on the outside, but the inside. One is willing and has certain beliefs, attitudes, and dynamics, and the other one has different things going on inside. As a result, the external "fruit" in life is very different. But, as Jesus taught, the fruit comes from the tree.

I talked recently to a married friend who went to stay with a single friend in New York for a few days. Aletha is an open, friendly, and emotionally available person. She likes men and has a lot of male friends. Men at work and in her social circles are always drawn to her. Her open heart invites them, and they sense she is warm and safe.

While in New York, Aletha and her friend went to several art exhibitions, many of which had social hours where you could hang around for food and drinks and meet the artists and other attendees. She laughed with her friend about how many men had come up to meet her and talk with her, not knowing she was married. She was being pursued at these functions when these men thought she was single. They were enjoying the humor of it all when her single friend blurted out, "Oh, that's just great. You are married, and they all want to ask you out, and that never happens to me."

"Well, have you tried smiling at them or going up to talk to them?" Aletha asked.

"I don't feel it's appropriate to flirt," her friend replied.

But Aletha told her it was bigger than flirting. "You have to give off vibes that you are an open person. Frankly, you seem 'bunkered down' and unavailable."

The single woman then went on to describe her internal world, her attitudes and thinking, and it was true. Although she never made the connection between her internal fears and reticence and the vibes she gave off, those fears bore negative fruit in her life.

Let me give you another example. Another friend of mine and I were talking about this problem when she told me a funny story. Christine is the wife of a pastor, and she grew up very guarded with men. Her mother always told her to "never smile or speak to a man you do not know. They will hit on you." For her entire adult life, she would always look the other way and avoid making eye contact with men. If her husband had not followed the advice in the chapter, "Where Is the Testosterone?" they would have never gotten married.

Christine and her pastor husband were on a trip, and she was waiting for him in the large open sitting area of the hotel. For some reason, she thought back to her mother's advice and decided, "That's ridiculous. I'm going to get past that. I'm tired of not being my normal friendly self, even to strangers." About that time, a man walked past, and she looked up at him, made eye contact, and said, "Hi," just as passers-by tend to do in friendly atmospheres. She remembered feeling, "See. That was nice. I was a normal member of the human race, and nothing bad happened." Proud of herself for growing past mom's warnings, she relished the moment and continued to people watch in the old hotel. Free at last!

A few minutes later, she saw the same man returning. He looked at her, smiled, sat down next to her, and struck up a conversation, asking her how long she was in town and so on. Although he seemed friendly and respectable, she freaked. "It's true!" she thought. "They are all out to get you! Mom was right." After the gentleman left, she had talked herself into not smiling any more—until she came to her senses.

But the point is clear. The state of someone's internal world of attitudes, openness, and fears has a lot to do with what happens in the outside world, especially in the world of dating. Christine had opened up her available heart, not for getting picked up but for connecting. And the outside world responded.

In the following chapters, we will embark on a journey that will do two things. First, if you have a "numbers problem" and you are not meeting any good people to date, you will get the numbers up by taking some active steps. But second, and the most important by far, you will take a hard look at internal attitudes, beliefs, fears, feelings, and religious blinders that might drastically affect your success level once you take steps to solve the numbers problem. To do that, I want you to convert to the belief that the outside world is affected by the inside. In other words, do two things right now:

1. Surrender your belief that the problem is that there are no good ones "out there," wherever "out there" is for you. Until you do, you don't get it and things won't change.
2. Join me in looking at the internal things and taking the action steps you can control that will open up new things "out there."

Sowing and Reaping

There is an old saying, "When the student is ready, a teacher will appear." That is another way of saying that life is about growth, and when we are ready for the next step in growth, we tend to find the necessary situation to teach us what we need to know, or change us in the way we need to be changed. Some of this is the natural law of sowing and reaping God has set up. But it is more than that too.

God himself will guide you into the next step of growth in your relational life, if you ask him. When you ask him how you need to change, God will bring you the wisdom and the circumstances that will help, and then you have to persevere in taking action. By taking those steps through even trying times like dating, God makes us "complete, lacking in nothing" (James 1:4).

You will find a consistent path in this book and in the system it teaches. The thinking is found in the Bible:

- God designs life and the good things he wants us to have, like relationships.
- We must step out to possess what he has created for us.

- When we do, we discover we are not ready or able to possess what we desire. In other words, our attempts will reveal where we need to grow.
- When failure happens and we find out where we need to grow, we ask God to help us, and we make the internal and external changes we need to make.
- We continue to persevere, and as we grow, we succeed in what he has created for us.
- We enjoy what he has provided and what we have grown into.

This is the path to building anything good in life. Sow, fail, learn, grow, sow, fail, learn, grow—and then you will reap. As Proverbs tells us:

> *The sluggard craves and gets nothing,*
> *but the desires of the diligent are fully satisfied.*
> *(Prov. 13:4)*

Sluggard means someone who "leans idly." In other words, sluggards are not active about their desires. Further word study reveals that sluggard means to "avoid pain." But those who are diligent take active steps (even if those steps are uncomfortable and painful at first) to change things about themselves and situations that are not bringing fruit, and they are fully satisfied. That is what I want you to see. Don't "lean idly" in your dating life and think the problem is the lack of good ones "out there." Take a look "in there," inside your heart, and get moving so that your desires are fully satisfied. Even if it takes a little work and some pain.

If you believe that the inside creates the outside, you are well on your way. So, get ready to dig up your relational "talents," invest them and put them to use, and watch God multiply you in the process. As you do that, you will discover the truth of stepping out, growing, and succeeding in all of life, including relationships.

Meet Five a Week

Okay, Lillie," I said. "Now that you have your log and we have a base-line of how it has been going, it's time for your second assignment."

"What is it?" she asked, with some excitement. She knew, now that the accounting was out of the way, we were ready to change her dating life.

"Every Friday, I want you to email me the names of five new men you have met that week that meet the three requirements we talked about:

1. They are new to you.
2. They have to have enough of an interaction with you to want to go out with you.
3. They have to have enough information about you to follow through on that desire.

"And do not fail to get five. Remember, I demand perfect obedience," I said.

"*What? Are you crazy?*" I can still hear her as she responded. "Where am I going to find five new men a week? I just told you I have not been finding any for two years, and you want five a week? Where am I going to meet them?" I could hear much exasperation and not a little contempt in her voice.

"Not my problem," I said. "Just make sure you get me my five names."

"But where, you freakin' psycho! Where am I going to meet five new guys a week? That's impossible."

"I don't know," I repeated. "Barnes and Noble? You go there a lot and browse. Starbucks? Guys come into there. Church? Certainly you don't know everyone who stands around after the service. The grocery store? The checkout line? At a restaurant? I don't care where you meet them. I just want you to find five that fulfill the three requirements."

"What in the world are you talking about? These will be perfect strangers. What would make you think they would even be guys I would want to go out with, or who would be good ones, or who would share my spiritual values? Especially at some of those places! How would I know what I was getting and how would I know I would want to go out with them?"

"*Stop!*" I said. "Who said anything about going out with them?"

"Well, you did," she said. "You said that they have to have enough information to ask me out and enough interaction to want to."

"Exactly. They do. You need to make that happen. But I didn't say you had to go out with them. I don't care if you ever see them again, much less go out with them."

"Well, why am I going to do this? How is that going to help if I never go out with them? How will that get me dates? Why would I do that?"

"Because I said so," I retorted. "Remember, I am the coach, and you have to do whatever I tell you. That's our deal."

I refused to tell her why at first because I knew my reasons would make no sense to her. Sometimes she would push hard for answers. One time I responded to an email from her with, "It would not be good for me to explain everything to you, Grasshopper!" I wanted her to "just do it." Initially, she would not understand why, but she had to obey.

Now she laughs at how important this particular assignment was in changing her life and ultimately to her getting married. In fact, she would say that without this step, she would probably still be single. So, let me explain what happened when she worked the assignment, and perhaps you can be won over as well.

First, she protested the impossibility of the assignment because she had a misconception about its purpose. She thought she had to find five men *she would be interested in*. To her, this meant that they had to have certain requirements, meet her tastes, be of the same values, and many other things. But this assignment was not about finding a good date, or a date at all (although it would eventually lead to that). I had absolutely zero interest in her getting asked out by any of these men.

The assignment was not about finding a man, but finding *herself*.

She had lost access to that part of herself that has to do with men and women connecting. In some ways she was inaccessible to men because parts of herself were inaccessible to her. As a result, she was not attracting men. She had lost the chemistry of interaction that comes from the soul.

She was cut off from things she did not know or understand. When she got in touch with all of herself, then all of that was available for others to connect with as well. That is the basis of a lot of good chemistry.

In addition, she lacked certain interpersonal skills of interacting with men. She was not in touch with that lack because she interacted very well with men at work and in other areas of life. But when one interacts with emotional connection as the desired outcome, as opposed to work, different dynamics come into play. I knew that, but I needed to get her moving so she could find that out for herself. She needed to meet new men and practice interacting. Then she would find out for herself the issues that were keeping her stuck.

First, she ran headlong into her passivity. She would see someone she did not know at a gathering, and she would think about talking to him to get one for her list of five. Then the first surprising discovery came.

"I was going to go talk to this guy, and I started to get really nervous inside," she called me to explain. "It was *weird*. I started to almost panic."

"What was that about?" I asked. I wanted to cheer, because I knew we had hit pay dirt. I wanted to say, teasingly, "Oh, I thought you didn't have any issues with men and this was just about God's not bringing the right one, or there not being any. Maybe you have been avoiding the very kinds of interaction that would bring one because you are afraid." But, being the good coach, I wanted her to find this out for herself. Since you are reading the book, you get to hear my internal "told you so's."

"I don't know," she said. "I was just scared. And there is no reason for it. I'm not interested in this person. I don't know him at all."

Nor do you know the one you will marry, when he comes along, I thought. *But if you have these same dynamics going on then, he will pass you by.* But I was getting ahead of myself, so I just said, "That's okay. Just keep going. Push through, strike up some conversations, and then monitor what is going on inside of you. I want to know what you are thinking when you get scared."

Being the good student, she pushed on. And she discovered something else: A lot was going on inside of her when she was interacting with men in a potential dating scenario. Let me give you an example of her initial discoveries.

"I was talking with this guy at church," she said, "He seemed nice and kind of attractive. I was drawn to him. But I started to feel that scared feeling and I noticed what I was thinking: *He thinks I'm fat. I'm coming across as stupid. He would never be interested in me.* And a bunch of other stuff was going through my head. I was so afraid of what he was thinking of me. I couldn't even be myself."

At that point, in my mind, *she had found her husband.* No, it wasn't this guy. But she found that part of her heart that would ultimately attract, interact with, win, and commit to her husband. She found the part of her that wanted to connect, but she feared rejection and other stuff from all the noise in her head. She had been unwittingly out of the dating game for a long time. Not intentionally, but just because she held back from getting out there, and when she was "out there," she was too repressed to attract the ones she wanted. She shut down, and the magic that happens between a man and a woman was not happening.

So, she took the necessary growth steps, which we will touch on in another chapter. She worked through the causes of those fears, practiced new ways of relating, was diligent in continuing to meet guys, and got to her promised land. *But she would have never done any of those things if she had not gotten moving.* She would still be channel surfing alone, I am sure. The cool thing was that meeting guys became fun for her; it became sort of a game in and of itself. She would call me on Thursday and beg, "I only have two! Give me some ideas."

"Okay, where are you?" I would ask. Then I would send her to Starbucks, to church, or to another office in her building. We laughed on many occasions about the scavenger hunt nature of my suggestions, the lame places she had to go, and the fun interactions she was having.

The same thing happened with another woman in her early thirties. She called me laughing hysterically at both herself and the guys she and her friends were meeting as they did the assignment together. They had discovered a whole new sport.

If you are like Lillie and don't even suspect that there may be things going on inside you that are keeping you stuck, just do the assignment for the sake of the numbers. Even if you do not buy into my "inside to outside" thinking, work on the outside. Get your numbers up. Meet new people. We will talk about ways to do that later, but either way, you have to get the numbers up—both to grow and to find dates.

I believe in good dating services as well as other methods for finding dates, but, please do this assignment as described here. Talk to people at church, your workplace, parties, and safe public places, on airplanes or buses, or wherever you find yourself. Return to the way you were in the safe, structured settings of high school or college where this kind of interaction happens naturally. As an adult, you have to make it happen for yourself.

You will find out a lot about your interpersonal skills and your fears, desires, defenses, and other parts of yourself that will become important to look at as you grow. Remember, this book is not just about growing your dating life. This book is about growing and healing your whole relational life, and as a result, your dating life will grow. Heal the tree, and the fruit will change.

A woman I am currently coaching found this out. I gave her the assignment to meet five guys a week, and she began doing it. She talked to the guy standing next to her in line at Starbucks, struck up a conversation with a guy in a restaurant, and chatted with another at a wedding. She was moving.

Then she said things started to happen to her. "Now they are talking to me!" she said. "I am doing *nothing*, and men are approaching me so much more and just interacting. It happened just today. I was at a restaurant, and this cute guy came up to me and started talking. We chatted for a long time and found out we know a lot of the same people. He's going to call me. The weird thing is that I'm not doing anything, and men seem to be responding to me more."

What she didn't know was that she *was* doing something. Working the assignment caused her to grow, become more available, and draw men to her. She became active, and her sowing was having its natural reaping effect. This is why two women can be standing at a party talking, and a man comes up and finds himself wanting to ask out one and not the other. Or why two guys can be talking to the same woman, and she is silently wondering about one and not the other. The difference is nothing you can see on the outside, but it is just as real. The chemistry is flowing again.

As we will see, chemistry is not all good, nor is it the ultimate test. *Don't ever make a commitment based only on chemistry.* There is such a thing as destructive chemistry. But what we are talking about here is the intangible, necessary chemistry of just being a person—a person who is open, interested, desiring of relationship, and not afraid. Taking the steps of this assignment will help to get that chemistry working again, or for the first time.

Action Steps

1. Find someone to be accountable to at the end of each week. Call, email, or meet for coffee and report to this person about the five men or women that fulfilled the three requirements.

2. Do it. Remember, all we are talking about is talking to the opposite sex long enough, anywhere, about anything, so that they would have a chance to be interested. This might be only a few minutes. Marriages begin that way. But you do not have to know you would be interested, know anything about them, desire any kind of further interaction, or follow through in any way. You just have to give them a chance to be interested in who you are.

3. Be very aware of your reactions: fears, judgments, devaluations of the people (he or she is too liberal, conservative, fat, skinny, tall, short), self-doubts, feelings, attractions, impulses, and the like. They will come in handy later in the program.

Expected Outcome

1. Getting yourself moving so that growth can take place.

2. Becoming aware of yourself and what you are like when you are trying to connect with the opposite sex.

3. Getting the numbers up and getting dates as a side benefit.

4. Learning more about the types you are not "attracted to" and those you are. You might find they even change lists!

8

Change Your Traffic Pattern

Keeping a log puts people in touch with their traffic patterns and the ruts they are in. Watching where they go, whom they talk to, whom they see over and over, and what groups they always frequent gives them a bird's-eye view into the reality of their dating life. Usually they realize this: While their patterns are serving many areas of life well, sometimes extremely well, they are not serving dating. And that is usually why they are stuck.

They may love their small group of friends, their work, or their church, and those areas of life are going very well. They would never think of abandoning them, nor should they. *The problem is that this traffic pattern is not exposing them to people who are eligible to date.* Then when they realize that the log does not show a random occurrence but a fixed pattern, they see the real problem. People fall into routines in life: same community, same recreation clubs, same church. That's good, but it doesn't serve dating very well.

Have you ever considered that you "have a pattern?" We all do. Just as I suggested you keep a log of the number of people you are meeting, I suggest you keep a log of your life and time. How are you spending it? Where do you go? Are you going anywhere new? Are you going places where there is an opportunity to meet someone new? How often? The log will help you to see how "out there" you are. It may be that you find you are really out there, and then you will know your problem is something different, like being more open. But you won't know until you observe your pattern.

So, don't abandon the things that are working for your life. But you have to realize that where you are spending your time is not serving dating either. If nothing is happening, continuing to do what you are doing pretty much ensures that nothing is going to happen. So do something different. What does this mean? It means to change your routine. Whatever that is, do some different things to serve dating. Go to some different places. You don't have to abandon your church, but you could visit another church at a different time than you normally go to yours, or switch services in your own church. The other day I heard a woman say that she had not known a particular man went to her church because "I always go to the 11:00 service." Routines are limiting.

Get real about whom you are meeting in the routines of your life. I am not suggesting that you reorient your entire life around dating. Dating should be a part of your life, not your life a part of dating. There is more to life than finding a date. But at the same time, dating is a part of your life, and if your "traffic patterns" don't include new people, they are not serving that part of your life.

What to Do

So, if your dating life is not working, where do you go?

I have already suggested that you consider a good dating service that matches you with people of your same faith, values, and interests (for more on this, see the next chapter, "Get over the Stigma: Join a Service"). But beyond that, what should you do? Based on talking with a lot of people and where they meet the ones they date, I can tell you the ways and places are limitless. They meet literally everywhere.

But the first key is this:

They go there more than once.

And the second key is this:

They keep going somewhere else if the first somewhere doesn't work.

People who meet people go where people are. And if they don't meet new people the first time they go, they *don't* embrace the sour attitude of "Oh, I tried that. It didn't work." Do you think that everyone who met their spouse at a party met him or her at the only party they ever went to? I know one woman who met her husband at the golf course. Think that was her first time to play golf? Or the only golf course she had ever been to? There are a million places where people meet people. But to meet new people, you have to be there.

Here are some places to meet people that I hear about frequently:

1. Visit churches. Churches are a great place to meet people with a spiritual life. But some people are often passive about church or a singles' group. If they are not meeting anyone at one church, they don't do anything about it, such as introducing themselves, visiting a different church, or joining a small group.

2. Talk to your friends (close and extended) about setting you up. Your friends know a lot of people. People get set up by friends, if they are telling their friends to be on the lookout for them, and if they tell their friends who know a lot of people and get around. There are three ways to do this. One is to get your friends to introduce you to someone in a safe setting, so you can see if you would like to go out. Another is the blind date. The third way is when a friend just tells another friend, "I know this great gal. The two of you would have a great time. Here is her number. I will call her and tell her you are going to call her." I just talked to a woman I am coaching today who is going out tonight with a new guy because a trusted friend gave him her number.

All three of these are okay, but you can probably guess my bias. Why not go out on either of the blind-date options? If you establish a rule that you will go out with anyone once (see Chapter 16, "Go Out with Almost Anyone Once, and Maybe Again," for a discussion of this rule), and you will be interacting with another human being, why not? If you don't like blind dates, make sure that does not indicate your pickiness, which may be keeping you stuck.

The big key here is twofold: You have to remind friends to be on the lookout in their circles, and you have to expand what you consider "friends" to set you up. These do not have to be your best friends. I am sure you know nice people who are not in your immediate circle to whom you could say: "Hey, keep me in mind with people you know or meet. I'm not meeting any new people." Many, many people are set up in that way with great results. It goes like this: "Hey, Susie. I work with this guy who is really nice, and I just thought of you. Want me to tell him to give you a call?"

I recently set someone up I had just met on a work project; I knew her very casually through a couple of business meetings and phone calls. She mentioned having moved to town after a break up, and I asked, "Are you dating anyone now?" She said no, so I told her I had a friend I would set her up with. They went out and had a great time. But I would not have thought to do that if he had not said to me a few weeks before, "Hey, if you meet anyone, keep me in mind." Don't be bashful. Seek referrals!

3. *Attend events sponsored by organizations.* You might not be that interested in what that organization is pushing at a particular event, but you might be interested in who might be interested! Charities, fund raisers, library lecture series, political events, community events, service events, galleries, and run-for-the-illness races are great ways to meet new people. Singles sometimes limit themselves to things they are involved in, as opposed to going other places where they might meet interesting people. Besides, you might surprise yourself and have a good time.

4. *Go to parties of all types.* Over and over again I hear, "We met at a party." Work gatherings, social gatherings, birthday parties, Super

Bowl parties, Oscar parties, parties for no good reason. If people are gathering, and if people are inviting people you do not know, go.

5. *Join organizations and activities related to your interests.* If you like biking, join a riding group. Books, a book group. Skiing, a club that takes trips. Softball, a league. Diving, a scuba group. Classical music, the donor circle at the symphony. Opera, friends of the opera. God has created a million different activities on the earth for you to enjoy. But the key is this: *Stop enjoying them solo or only with the people you already know.* Branch out and do the things you love with larger groups and associations. Your career path probably has lots of seminars you don't attend. Maybe it's time to go to some.

6. *Check the newspaper and web.* Most papers have local activities postings, at least as the weekend approaches. Commit to going together with a friend to a certain number of events per month. Hold yourself to it, with your team, in the same way you would be accountable to going to the gym.

7. *Throw some parties.* You don't have to wait for others to have a party. Get a group together and have your own. Have a barbecue and get your friends to invite people they don't usually hang out with, and expand your circle. I have a friend who every Christmas throws a party and hands out invitations to all his guy friends and tells them to all invite three single women they are not dating. Many, many people met other singles they had never met before. Lots of dates came from that event, and someone I know well met his wife there.

8. *Start something up.* I know a group of women who used to host a monthly event called SWARM (Single Women Actively Recruiting Men, as they affectionately called themselves). They had fun events every month, such as dances, dinners, and boat outings. New people met new people at these events, and they were a lot of fun. I applauded them for their creativity and being active. The guys I talked to loved that the women were so up front about the activities being for meeting people.

9. *Seek out and attend cultural events.* You love art, music, and museums, but do you go to the events surrounding those interests?

What about the fund raisers or the "meet the artist" gatherings? If you are into the arts at all, there are usually a lot of activities that support them. Go online, or look in the paper at what is available. If you are into literature, attend book signings of your favorite authors at bookstores.

10. Visit single vacation and recreational spots. You know the single spots in your area of the country. Why not get a few friends together and go where the singles go? There are probably more at a great beach town or ski town than at Grandma's. Come on, you need a vacation anyhow. This does not have to be expensive either. Share lodging and get a cheap fare. Get moving. Also, go on more than one big vacation. Do a lot of little weekend things. I just talked to a woman who went on a weekend wine-tasting trip and met her new honey. Another one met someone on a river-rafting weekend.

Get out there and do the things you love in places where other singles go. Look at group outings that local associations sponsor, such as dive trips from a diving shop, or ski trips from a ski shop. Just get moving in activities you enjoy instead of doing it your regular way.

11. Exercise at the place where they are. Some gyms are attended by the narcissistic self-worshipers; others are where the normal people go. Instead of jogging around your block, maybe it is time to fork out a few bucks and go where the regular working people get in shape. Your local recreation department may have less expensive Pilates, aerobics, or kick-boxing classes.

12. Take a class. A great way to meet motivated, interesting people not in your normal circle of friends is to take classes. I know one woman who took a course in oriental exercise because she knew nothing about it, and months later she still gets together with the people from her class. These friends ended up setting her up. Many such courses are short and inexpensive. Business-related, skill-related, arts, and self-improvement classes are all available. Check the listings at your local community colleges or universities or other organizations that offer classes. You might even meet a new friend there who knows someone.

13. Join your coworkers when they go out. The old "Well, I don't want to meet someone at a bar" usually means, "I don't want to go just get picked up for sex." Of course you don't, and I would not want you to do that either. But, at the same time, many people have thrown out the baby with the bath water. There are many respectable places where good, normal, responsible, value-driven, social people gather with friends after work or on weekends. What is wrong with going with your friends to the equivalent of a "mixer" for adults?

If you can't control yourself in some way, or if you are vulnerable to substance abuse or sexual addiction and might do something impulsive, then don't go. But, if you have self-control and maturity, why not join your friends who will be meeting other friends and people you don't know? Good, upscale places where good people gather are great places to mingle with other professionals or working people. Remember, you can be in the world without being of it, as Jesus was. Don't be afraid of social gatherings unless there is a good reason to be. Rigid rules only have an appearance of wisdom (Col. 2:20–23) but have nothing to do with spiritual maturity.

"That Will Never Work"

Okay, I caught you. I know what you're thinking, because I have had it said to me by people I have coached:

- "That won't work. I will never meet anyone at a charity gathering."
- "I have gone to all the good churches."
- "I have been in a softball league. They are all a bunch of loser jocks."
- "No one worth meeting goes out after work."
- "Only geeks go to book signings."
- "There will only be ten people there."

I have heard all the excuses. But here is the thing: You may have tried some of these ideas, but you may not have been as active as I suggest you be, nor were you working the program you are about to learn about. This is a whole new world. There is a chance you have never truly been "out there." So, don't let your excuses hold you back any longer. These are the places where people do meet the ones they date. Keep trying.

The other day I talked to a friend about this book, and she said, "Oh, my! I have a single friend who needs to read it because it is so clear why she is still single. She goes to one or two events and then says, 'See, it never works. You never meet anyone at stuff like that.' When I was single, I would go to everything, all the time. That is the only way you ever meet people. And, she is *so* picky. She won't even go out with anyone if he doesn't meet some preset standard in her head."

Then my friend said something even more telling. "You know, it's interesting," she said, thinking out loud. "It is only my single friends who think like that. None of my married friends were that way when they were dating. We all went out to anything, and with lots of different kinds of people, and they were not so picky. Now we all miss it! My single friends need to not be so picky and go to everything, just as my married friends once did. There is a lesson in that."

I could not have agreed more with her observations, and she had not even coached anyone. She had just noticed that the ones who found someone they love were the ones who did not let defenses and excuses keep them locked up in small worlds. If you don't believe me, ask the people you know who are married or in a relationship where they met the person. Usually it will have been in some small, insignificant place, event, or way. But they went there.

So get creative, get active, and change lanes!

Here's a good way to do that: Keep a log and observe yourself. Have you ever considered that you "have a pattern"? We all do. Just as I suggested that you keep a log of the number of people you are meeting, I suggest you keep a log of your life and time. How are you spending it? Where do you go? Are you going anywhere new? Are you going anywhere where there is a chance of meeting someone? How often? The log will help you to see how "out there" you are. You may find you are really out there, and then you will know your problem is something different, such as being more open. But you won't know until you observe your pattern.

9

Get Over the Stigma: Join a Service

Y ou've got to be joking," Lillie said. "There's no way I'm joining an online dating service. That is so desperate. That's for people with absolutely no life."

"So, Miss 'My-Dating-Life-Is-Going-So-Well, I Won't Do What You Say,' how is it working your way?" I countered.

"Horrible, but there has to be another way. I'm not going to be some internet love affair for the Unabomber. That is so sick."

"Get serious. It doesn't work that way."

"But it's so *unnatural*. It's so *unromantic*. I don't want my love story to be 'we met on the internet.' How gross!"

"Fine. Sit at home. It's your life. But before you say no, just listen to what I have to say. Maybe you will get another take on it."

I went on to give her my experience with people whose dating life was stagnant and my theory on why services can be a great solution. After hearing it, she began to see it differently, as I hope you do as well.

A Genuine Problem

When Lillie kept a log on how many new men she was meeting, the numbers were depressing. Remember her first answer? Zero.

As we have seen, most of that was an internal problem. She had to work on internal dynamics that were keeping her stuck. But as we have also said, she did have a real *numbers* problem. How can you date if you are not meeting anyone new? Also, on the flip side, how can you work through your issues and practice if you are not meeting people? So, my first suggestion to her was that she had to change her traffic pattern and go where the men are. (See chapter 8, "Change Your Traffic Pattern.") She had to get her numbers up.

But my next suggestion was that she join a service. She argued with me, as we have just seen. Her reasons revolved around what she considered the stigma of online dating. Some people feel as if you have to be a loser, a sex addict, or a socially inept person to find dates on the internet. Others are opposed to any kind of online dating, thinking that something has to be wrong with you if you can't find dates "on your own." But that is not true. Every day, good services match good people together. Some of them are internet based and some are not.

My theory of why these are needed now is *not* that people are desperate. There are real reasons why adults have a hard time finding other adults to date. Life is different from what it used to be. Here are some things to think about before you decide whether to join a service.

1. Adulthood is a time of life that lends itself less to meeting people to date. When people are in college, for example, they are thrown together on a campus with several thousand eligible people of the same age, demographic, and expectations. Every day, they have the opportunity to participate in tons of activities where they can meet someone new. Meeting new people is part of the college culture; approaching someone and saying, "Hi, I'm Jessica," is just part of school life. It doesn't seem at all like approaching a stranger in the adult world, where the person did not go to that baseball game to be approached by a stranger. It is just different.

In addition, there are structured mixers between groups, sororities, fraternities, organizations, and clubs designed to help students meet other students, make new friends, and find dates. If someone is not dating in school, it almost *has* to be an inner dynamic problem, for there is so much opportunity.

Usually, right after college or high school, the single culture continues to flourish. Friends remain friends, and they are all still in touch with each other. They socialize frequently and bring new friends into the mix. They have parties, go to clubs together to have fun, and do activities as groups. This continues for a few years, but then something happens.

About the mid to late twenties, the cohesion of that kind of community and of that kind of attitude begins to break apart. You see less of the big-group stickiness, and people's lives get more segmented. Many of them have gotten married and have dropped out of the club, so to speak. Others have gotten buried in their work. The group mentality slowly gives way to people living more "away from the group," individual lives. This is not purposeful; it just happens as life goes on. The problem is that *there is no structure to replace the one that school offered and early adulthood continued.* The social structure from the younger years sunsets, and people are now thrown full-fledged into the world of work.

Some have jobs where they meet new people, and they do better. Others, like Lillie, work with the same people every day. Since they do not call on people outside the company, they never meet anyone new. Each night they go home to their roommate or to an empty apartment; on Saturday they run errands, and on Sunday they go to the same church. Adult life has sentenced them to seeing the same people they always see. No new date possibilities. The old structured environments that provided a constant flow of new faces has disappeared. They are trapped in a dateless desert.

One woman told me once, "I had a depressing Fourth of July. It was so different from four or five years ago. Then, I was part of a big group of thirty or forty people who always hung out and brought new friends. Meeting people just happened. Now members of the group have just drifted apart. This year there were twelve people, and all but my girlfriend and I were 'coupled.' It is more and more like that the further into adulthood I get."

What college and other structures used to provide in the way of meeting people, a service can do now. It is not for desperate people; it is just a structured way to meet new people. It does the same thing a mixer used to do when you were in school.

2. *In our transient society, the structure of community itself has broken down.* Community itself seemed to be more cohesive in days gone by. People moved less, communities were not as mobile. As a result, everyone knew everyone, and connections were more easily made. You were more likely to know someone who knew someone who had a nephew who was single and who might be a good match for you. There was a party coming up, and they made sure that the two of you met. Or they just introduced you or set you up. There was a little more of a bird's-eye view of a cohesive community, and connections were more easily made. Everyone knew the town "match-maker," and she was usually successful.

Today, people are more mobile, and there are fewer and fewer of those kinds of communities. Jobs move people, technology makes everything go faster and become more fragmented, and the days of ice cream socials, where there was a network that introduced everyone to everyone in town, are gone. There is less of a cohesive community to know all the eligibles and put them together. Your friends don't know your friends.

This does not mean that people do not have "community," but their communities are not connected. I have talked to many singles who have different groups of friends and support systems that do not know each other. This gives them many fragmented "pools" to date from, but not a larger cohesive one in which members have a greater opportunity of connecting with each other for your benefit.

As adults, people get stuck in their routines, and they see the same people over and over. Many churches, offices, and other places where singles hang out do not have a high influx of new people. Singles tend to see the same people over and over again.

Many people work in small businesses, with fewer employees. In larger organizations, people often "get segmented" in their own corner of the universe. Work takes up many hours a week. If it is not the kind of work where you are out meeting people in the outside world, it works against your finding people to date.

Many Christian singles almost exclusively look at church singles groups as the place to find people to date. That does not seem to work for many people, and besides that, it is not a good motivation to go to a singles' group. A singles' group is first and foremost a spiritual community where members are taught God's ways, supported in their faith, and given an opportunity to serve. When people make it their only avenue for finding dates, they are often disappointed. This does not mean you can't find dates there, but the feedback I get is that attending singles' group meetings can turn into a routine that does not produce dates.

Other life routines create the same traffic pattern rut. Every week, people spend time in the same ways, they frequent the same places, and they hang out with the same people. It is like going to the same refrigerator time after time, looking for food, but knowing that fifteen minutes ago you opened it up and did not find any. If you want to eat, you need to get in the car and go get some food!

So, given these realities, why not join a service designed to do something about your problem of not meeting anyone? What is there to lose? Time? Effort? You might not like everyone you meet? I hope you have gotten past that attitude by now. You are going to have to invest the time, kiss a few frogs, and meet a lot of people to go through the changes we are talking about and get the numbers working on your side. Sowing and reaping. What do you have to lose if your goal truly is to gain experience and have experiences?

So, I sold Lillie on the idea. She did not like it, but she did it. Guess what? She met her husband on an online dating service that matched people by compatibility measures and not just some fake personal ad and a ten-year-old-and-thirty-pounds-lighter photo. It was reputable and based on a psychological profile each member had to complete. Lillie and her husband-to-be found they had a lot in common, and they corresponded. Finally they had a face-to-face meeting. Now I'm waiting to hear when the kids are coming. If she had listened to her own "stigma talk," there would have been no marriage.

Hints

Here are a few hints on using a dating service:

1. Remember, this is about getting your numbers up. Don't get discouraged if you do not find the "one" immediately. Meet a lot of people.
2. Do not quit too soon. I have talked to many people who gave up because they did not immediately get a "match." Or they went out with a few who did not meet their expectations. Just let the numbers do their work.
3. Research the available services and see which one focuses on the kinds of people you are looking for. Talk to some people in your area who have used it and ask them how it went.
4. Don't limit yourself, when you create your profile, with a rigid list of requirements and expectations.
5. Always be careful. Make sure you go through the proper channels. Find out about a person's network of friends, work, and community. Meet in a public place, get proper information, and get to know someone before giving someone personal information or being alone with him or her. Do not put yourself at risk. Contact the service itself and find out about its safety practices. Stay safe.

There are a number of other ways to get your numbers up, which we will talk about later. But dating services, online and others, can be a great tool. Using technology and professional networking will help you go through a lot of people quickly to find some who interest you. They are one more tool in the arsenal.

The more I have been attuned to the problem of finding dates over the recent years, the more I keep hearing success stories of people who met their dates and mates there. You never know, but it may be worth a try. If you get past your reservations about it, you might find what Lillie and others have found: There are other good people like you who need some help meeting new people.

10

Stick With It, and Get Your Numbers Up

My married friend Kristin asked me what book I was writing. When I told her, she immediately started talking about a friend of hers.

"My friend Meredith needs to read your book. She is so stuck in her dating life. At thirty-four she is so cynical about dating, but what she does is a joke. She will never get married the way she goes about it.

"The other night she called me. She had just gone out on a date with a guy she had met through a dating service. She had been unhappy with her dating life, and we had been on her case to do something about it. She always does the same thing. She has this little list of requirements she is looking for, and if someone wants to set her up with someone and he does not fit her 'list,' she says no. She is never going to find someone that way.

"So, we talked her into joining this service, and she had just had her first date. Now she is quitting the service because she said he's a loser. I don't have any hope for her. The funny thing is that she dates *nothing like I did or my married friends did when they were dating.*"

"What do you mean?" I asked.

"Well, it seems as though my friends who are married were not so boxed in with all of these little requirements. We just dated a lot of people, then we got 'surprised' by someone. We went on a *lot* of dates. Bad ones. Losers. People we weren't interested in. We all did. You aren't going to find out who you like without going out with some you don't like. And, it's like anything else in life, you have to stick with it."

"Will you write that chapter for me?" I asked. "I wish every single person could hear what you just said. It was exactly the advice the other married woman in the Traffic Pattern chapter gave."

"Well, they should talk to us married women. We know that the prince doesn't just fall out of the sky. You have to kiss a lot of frogs. And what is really funny is you end up falling for one that is *nothing* like what you thought you wanted, or the kind that you always used to go for. My husband is that way, and so are the husbands of a lot of my married friends."

True words, I thought. So I want to reiterate them here.

Remember earlier when I said that it is not primarily a numbers problem? That is, internal issues keep people single as much as not having enough good prospects? I talked a lot about working on the internal issues that may be holding you back, even from finding prospects. Well, sticking with it and getting your numbers up is *both* an inside *and* an outside issue.

To find dates worth keeping, you must get your numbers up (an outside issue). Dating is primarily a numbers game, even though there are exceptions. You will occasionally hear stories such as these: "I married the first person I went out with in college," or "I married my high school sweetheart." This is not the norm. People usually go through a lot of people to find good relationships. That's just the way it is.

To get your numbers up, you have to be willing to stick with it (an inside issue). If you are easily discouraged because you had a bad date, you might get stuck and give up too soon. If a particular dating service does not work for you in the first few tries, you bail out on it. Or you quit trying altogether. To get your outside numbers up, you have to deal with all of your internal messages that keep you from doing it.

Just the other day I talked to two people about the same Christian online dating service. One was so negative on it she had given up. "I got matched with losers," she said (which probably means two men she didn't like). The other one was so high on it because she had found her boyfriend there. But she had dated several people, even in other cities. She did not connect with the first few she contacted. The interesting thing was that these two women had had virtually the same experience, and one was happy and the other disillusioned. To one, after a handful of bad dates, the glass was still half full. To the other, it was empty. Same glass, different outcome.

This is not just about dating. It is this way with all of life. People who make life work rarely hit home runs the first time at bat. They strike out, hit a few foul balls and a single here and there, and slowly they win the game. Success at anything in life works this way. It is a numbers game, with constant improvement along the way. People's stick-to-it *attitude* is what leads to their success.

I repeat that this issue is both an internal and an external one. The external part is that you have to get your numbers up. You have to do things that get you introduced to and to go out with a lot of different people. Get your numbers up, even if you have to join a service. Get them up, get them up!

The internal part is that to get your numbers up, *you can't give up when things don't go well.* If you get discouraged and quit, then by definition your numbers are going to be low. To get to a lot of people, you have to keep going—even when you do not like the results or are not interested in the ones you are finding. Keep going. Anyone can get excited about the beginning of a plan or working a program, like people do on New Year's Day about their resolution to get in shape. They start out well, for about a week or two. Then they quit, *even though they have already done what works.* They have shown that they can do it, but they don't keep doing it. *The winners do what a lot of the losers did, but they just keep doing it.*

As Solomon said, "The end of a matter is better than its beginning, and patience is better than pride" (Eccl. 7:8). The beginning is easy to do, but having the patience to actually go to the end is a whole different matter.

First, you have to stick with it. This is why Kristin compares her married friends to her friend who has no dates. They had the patience to kiss a lot of frogs, and they got to the end of their frog-kissing days through a lot of perseverance. If you are having fun learning about yourself and others, and are having fun experiences because you have made dating "not about marriage," what's the problem? There is nothing lost, and you are gaining experience. Keep going and stick with it. What else were you going to be doing that night? I am convinced people have "bad dates" often because they expect to find a soul mate instead of enjoying an experience with an interesting person. Just have fun instead of demanding that every date bring you love.

Second, you have to have something to stick with. So I will say it again, *this is a numbers game.* You have to sow to reap. Do the things we talked about in the chapter about changing your traffic pattern. Go where the people are. Get involved and take the little steps that, all added up, lead to a lot of people. In my experience, what I have seen about dating is what I see about people who succeed in other areas as well. They are involved, active, and looking for small opportunities, not the home run. Keep going to the places where people go—even if you do not think they will help.

In reality, when you ask people where they met their spouses, they give answers that show the most *common*, nondramatic activities. Here are examples of where couples I know met each other:

- church
- party
- convention
- organizational event
- museum
- sports event
- diving class
- professional event
- work (colleagues, clients, etc.)
- library
- book club
- dating service
- school
- graduate school

- volunteer work
- wedding
- airplane
- blind date
- alumni event
- family member
- friend

I could go on and so could you. If you listed all the married people you know and where they met, you would find that for the most part they met in ordinary ways. Go ask them.

There are exceptions, but even those happen in ordinary places. I have a friend who was on a plane, and a man stepped on. When he did, she said that God said to her, "That is the man you are going to marry." She had never heard anything like that before, but swears this is what happened. I know her well, and she is not the type that "hears voices."

The guy sat down several rows in front of her, and she shrugged off what had happened, thinking she was nuts. She turned back to her magazine, questioning her sanity.

About an hour into the flight, the guy got up, came back, and asked if he could sit next to her! He said he had noticed her when he got on the plane, and he wanted to meet her. After they had talked for a while, he asked if he could take her out when they got to their destination. She told him she was a Christian and he needed to understand her values. She would go out with him, but there would be no "funny stuff." They went out once, had a good time, and agreed to meet again.

To make a long story short, he came to visit her in her hometown, where she still lived. She took him to meet her parents, and her father explained to him what faith in Jesus was. He became a Christian through her father. A year later, they got married. That was twenty years ago.

Even dramatic stories occur in nondramatic settings, and they occur through being *open* and *active*. What was it about her that said to him, "She is open enough that I can go sit by her"? Then when he came back to sit next to her, her openness kept him interested and even got him more interested.

Even in the extraordinary cases like this one, people meet in everyday events, doing the things we talk about in this book. Dates are found where people are. Go where the people are, even if that is mundane. Be open, get your numbers up, and stick with it.

Then, as a further reminder, be creative (as we said earlier). Join a service, go to events, and make your own events. The more numbers, the better. Sow, and you will reap. That is the name of the game, and then God will send rain and make it grow:

> *Cast your bread upon the waters,*
> *for after many days you will find it again.…*
> *Sow your seed in the morning,*
> *and at evening let not your hands be idle,*
> *for you do not know which will succeed,*
> *whether this or that,*
> *or whether both will do equally well.*
> *(Eccl. 11:1, 6)*

Let me end with a story I heard at a conference at which I recently taught. A man from New York lost his wife to illness a number of years ago. He decided it was time to start dating again, but he wasn't getting anywhere with the traditional methods of dating, so he joined an internet dating service.

At first he cast his net close to the boat, and he didn't meet anyone he was interested in pursuing. He widened his search, still with no success. He finally widened his net to include the whole country, and he was matched with a woman in Oregon. It was his best and most interesting match. He started corresponding with her, and soon they were talking on the phone. The more they shared, the more they found they liked each other. He flew to Oregon to meet her face to face, and after that trip their relationship deepened.

They made many such trips over the next several months, and before long, they knew they wanted to be together. Today they are married.

He experienced much discouragement in dating at the beginning, and he was not finding anyone. Nevertheless, he kept with it, as did she. Perseverance, through discouragement, wins the prize.

11

Get Your Team Together

> *Two people can accomplish more than twice as much as one; they get a better return for their labor. If one person falls, the other can reach out and help. But people who are alone when they fall are in real trouble.*
>
> *(Eccl. 4:9–10, NLT)*

On and off for close to a year Gretchen had been in a relationship with one of those men with whom you would not want to build a home. There were many reasons why she needed to break it off with Ryan, but she had a big problem. Every time she would break up with him, he would turn on the charm to get her back, and she would go back and start it all over again.

Gretchen joined a small growth group of some other women who held each other accountable in areas where they were trying to grow. She told them of her pattern of breaking up and going back with her boyfriend Ryan. They confronted her on the destructiveness of the pattern and how she was being used and would never find what she wanted if she did not get out of that relationship for good. Shortly after she joined the group, she allowed Ryan to lure her back one more time. The members of the small group worked on her and worked on her. Finally she got the courage to end it for good.

This time was different. When she and Ryan had broken up in the past, she would get depressed and sad, thinking that they would never be together again. This thought devastated her; she loved so much about him. But this time, the group had prepared her for the breakup.

"When you break up with him, you are going to do it right before we meet. We will be there for you afterwards," they told her.

So she did. She broke up with Ryan and met with her small group, and they balanced the depressing reality of the loss. She even stayed for a few nights with one of the women in the group to get through her "withdrawals." Each day, she got a little stronger and less tempted to return Ryan's calls. But this was not the biggest victory.

A few weeks later, Ryan did catch her on the phone one night. They talked to "just catch up." The more they talked, the more she remembered all the things about him she liked—his humor, intelligence, sensitivity (at least for short bursts). No one could make her feel like he did. She was softening.

That is when he said, "Why don't you come over? It would be so good just to catch up . . . I miss you."

She hesitated, but she too was caught up in the moment. *It sounds like he might have changed*, she thought. *It is worth one more try*, she told herself.

"Okay," she said. "Give me a little while to get dressed, and I'll be right over." She hung up the phone, and she felt excited and a little afraid. But then it happened.

As she told the group later, "I was getting excited about seeing him and hopeful that things would be different, that the breakup had forced him to get committed and turn things around. But, as I was getting dressed, I started to hear things! And it was you guys. This is what I heard you say:

"'What are you doing? He is just going to use you again.'

"'Don't sleep with him, like you do when you are weak and then hate yourself the next morning.'

"'Every day spent with him is a day keeping you from the right one.'

"'Find someone who respects you and treats you like you really want to be treated.'

"'He will never be the spiritual leader you want.'

"It was as if all of you were in the room with me. I did not have a chance!" she laughed. "And I came to my senses. I had done this too many times—out of loneliness and the false hope of his seductive charm I would give in to another failure. But this time, I didn't. I called him and told him I wasn't coming and to not call me again. It was over. *And I owe it all to the strength you gave me.*"

She successfully broke up and now is happily married to a good man.

Joel was a really good guy whom everybody liked. His married friends, especially the women, could never understand why he was still single at thirty-five. He seemed to be such a catch, so he took a lot of ribbing.

Although he wanted to be in a good relationship, he tended to idealize a woman from afar and be passive about going for her. He would get up his courage and ask her out. Usually the woman would say yes, and they would go out and have a good time.

But then, one of two things would happen. Either she would really fall for him, and he would lose interest, or he would get smitten, and the woman would lose interest in him. He had a pattern of not getting the one he wanted and keeping the one he did not want too long.

Thankfully, he got a group of people together who were committed to his growth, and he put his dating out on the table. He told them that he wanted to hear all that they had to say about him and his dating life and that he would try to act on their feedback.

When he did that, two things happened. First, his team members found out that he was too scared to tell someone that he was not interested in her. He could not say, "I think you are a very nice person, but I don't think I want to pursue dating further. I don't think this is the kind of relationship I want." He was afraid of hurting a woman's feelings. So they confronted him and forced him to be clearer with the "hangers on"—the women whom he would continue to go out with past when it was clear he should move on.

Second, they found that with a woman he liked, he turned into a big "people-pleaser." He was not all of himself (see chapter 20, "Be Yourself from the Beginning"). This woman did not see the real Joel, with all of his assertiveness, charm, and power. Instead, she saw a little boy trying to please. Little turns a woman off more than feeling as though she has all the power in a relationship, so, naturally, she would lose interest, and he would feel devastated.

Joel and his group of friends were working through the *Boundaries in Dating* workbook (coauthored by John Townsend and me), and they began to challenge his patterns. He had to get stretched in some ways. He became more assertive, both with the ones he did not want as well as the ones he did. They challenged him to step out sooner, and he took more risks. He gave up the passive gaze from afar and made his move sooner. He was growing up.

Then, he met a woman whom he really liked, and he was ready. He was himself—assertive, stepping out, charming, *and* scared to death! But his group walked with him through it, through the "she will never like me" and "she is probably looking for someone way more attractive and accomplished than me." They told him to shut up and get back in there, like a trainer in a boxer's corner. He did, and now he and Gail have three kids, a mortgage, the picket fence, and all that comes with finding "the one."

But one thing is certain. If it had not been for his "team," helping him gain insight, confronting him, building him up, encouraging him, and pushing him past his limits, he would still be gazing from afar, or in a relationship going nowhere for way too long. Thank God for his team.

I know a woman whose friends did the same thing as Gretchen's, but this woman would not listen. In fact, she got angry at them. Two years after her wedding, she got divorced. Part of putting a team together is being willing to listen to and act on the team's feedback. This does not mean your team is always right or always understands the whole picture. They may judge someone wrongly. But it does mean you have to be open *with them* to discovering the truth about your dating relationship, for they are the ones who know and love you best. Do not do dating alone.

Attitude check: You cannot change your dating life alone. Admit that you need a good support system to help you grow in this area of your life.

Action Step: Put Your Team Together

The team you assemble depends on what you need. It could be a therapist, a small group, recovery group, prayer partners, accountability partners, a therapy group, a mentor, or wise friends. There is no hard and fast rule. The only rule is that you must make yourself vulnerable to them, submit to them, put it all out there for them to see, and consider the wisdom, feedback, challenges, and correction they offer you.

In chapter 13 ("Don't Limit Yourself to a Type"), you'll see what happened to Lillie when she took active steps to change her dating life. Things shift, and you begin to change and grow internally. This can be scary at times, it can bring you to the end of your own strength and resources, and you will need help. When that happens, where are you going to get it?

I guarantee you (and Lillie would too) that without the team she put together, she could not have gone through the process she needed to go through and make the changes she needed to make. They were the key ingredient to the plan working. So think about yourself: When you hit the tough places in the path of dating and the changes you need to make, where are you going to get that help? Here are some things you will need as you walk the dating path:

- wisdon
- correction
- support
- courage
- prayer
- honest, brutal feedback
- insight
- self-awareness
- discernment of your date's character
- prodding to take risks

- a push to try again
- modeling
- encouragement
  to get up

- confrontation and limit-setting
- suggestions and strategy
- alternative voices to
  the ones in your head

All these things your group can provide. Just remember, no one ever accomplished great things by themselves, especially in the arena of personal growth. Get your team together.

12

Tie Me to a Tree

My friend Dan was divorced a few years ago, and I knew exactly what he would do after the divorce: He would find another woman right away and begin dating her exclusively. It would happen fast, and he would not see it coming. So I warned him about this tendency, and I recommended that he commit to at least six months of no dating. He could hang out with friends, but nothing that looked like dating. Then, I suggested he date after that with the commitment to not get exclusive for at least another six months. I also made a rule for him that he had to be going out with at least five different women at any one time. Not in serious relationships, but just dating. He had to tell everyone that he was not interested in any romantic commitment but was just having fun going out with a lot of different people.

But Dan did not take my advice, and what I feared would happen, happened. A woman came along and told him how wonderful he was. "She was so positive!" he said, referring to the contrast between her and his ex-wife, who he said was negative toward him most of the time. "She really appreciates who I am." Dating her was like pouring balm on a wound.

Dan started hanging out with her almost exclusively. He was well on his way to comfort city without having dealt with anything that caused his divorce. He was facing neither the grief from his divorce nor his problems in choosing women. He looked like a sheep headed for the slaughter.

But, fortunately for him, I and a couple of close friends got on his case and "tied him to a tree."

We intervened and told him, "Look, you are young and have your whole life ahead of you, but you have some serious vulnerabilities. Any time a woman thinks you are a good guy, you believe it! You get hooked by her, take the bait, and are caught. If you do that here, you will never work through the things you need to work through to have a good marriage. So we are not going to let you do this. Call this woman and tell her you are finished!"

He tried to deny that the relationship was serious, but we didn't care. It was what it was, and we knew he was not dealing with his life and his issues. He was following an old, unhealthy pattern, and as his friends, we were not going to let him do that.

He listened, knowing that we cared for him. And he followed our suggestions. He went six months with no dates. He got into divorce recovery, saw a therapist, and worked on all of his issues. Then he began to date and promised not to commit to anyone for six months. He promised to date a lot of women and to learn from the experience.

After about a year of dating around, he found a wonderful woman and committed to her. She was a good choice. But, here is the point: *It would never have happened had we not tied him to the tree.* Without his supportive friends who were committed to his well-being, he would have allowed his auto-pilot ways to rule him, and he would have made another bad choice.

"Tie me to a tree" means you empower a team of people to confront you and prevent you from falling into self-destructive behaviors.

Tell them what your patterns have been and give them permission to stop you when you fall into those patterns. Tell them what your weaknesses are and ask them to step in when you display weakness. This is police work at its finest. As the Bible says, the law is for the lawless (1 Tim. 1:9). If there are parts of you that do not operate according to the laws of what is good and healthy for you, then get the sheriffs to step in and arrest you. Below are just a few examples of when you might need your team to confront you. They will confront you when you do any of the following:

- Make excuses for not working your plan
- Go for the wrong type for the one thousandth time and think that this time it is going to be different
- Know you need to break it off with a person who is not good for you
- Do break off a bad relationship, but are tempted to go back or actually do go back into the relationship
- Break up or divorce, and you need to heal and grow instead of getting right back into something exclusive "on the rebound"
- Deviate from the plan you are working
- Shrink back from growth steps you are supposed to be taking
- Get involved with someone who is not of good character
- Date seriously someone who does not share your faith
- Give up your morals for the person you are dating
- Unplug from your spiritual life and friends while dating
- Are smitten by someone who has some serious issues
- Are being two people in the relationship to get the person to like you

At these times, strong needs or feelings inside have overcome your rational faculties and you need to be chaperoned. This is why I said early on that you need to get your team together before dating. If they are there and empowered, they can act. They are on your side. Do not fight them, and listen to what they have to say. They may save your dating life.

13

Don't Limit Yourself to a Type

Lillie and I continued our conversations as she worked the program. The next obstacle she encountered could well have been faced by Sarah or Sydney, Rich or Sam, or several others who were in my dating groups. I see the same problem over and over.

I asked Lillie about some of the guys she currently knew. One man's name was mentioned, and she commented, "He's nice. But I would never go out with him."

"Oh, yeah?" I asked. "Why not, especially if he's nice?"

"He's just not my type."

"What do you mean?"

"Well, I go for taller, more athletic guys. He's more of the business type. I mean, he's smart and all that, but not the type I like."

"Tell me more about your 'type.'"

"I like the strong athletic type and someone who is spiritually mature and outgoing, stuff like that. I thought I had met one like that not long ago, but I didn't like some of his theological perspectives or his politics."

"So, let me get this straight," I said. "For you to go out with someone, they have to pass a prescreening checklist in your head, including physical type, theology, and politics?" I knew Lillie had strong political as well as theological views.

"Sure. I mean I could never go out with anyone who was a *liberal.*"

"I think the FedEx man is looking better all the time," I quipped. "I haven't even heard all of your requirements yet, and you're already really, really limiting the field. You are *nuts* in the way you think about this, if you want my opinion."

"Why do you say that?" she asked with the hint of contention that had become normal for many of our interactions.

"For several reasons. *Several* reasons."

"Like what?" she pressed. "You are not saying I have to try to fall for someone I would not be into, are you? I have heard that stuff before, and I can't do that. Just choose to love someone you are not that into. Yuck."

"No, I would not say that either. I would never, ever want you to 'try' to like anyone you did not like. That's stupid. I think you should find someone you really like, someone who really turns you on in every way," I reassured.

"So, why would you want me to go out with someone I am not attracted to? It seems like a waste of time."

"Well, other than the fact that *your* system does not seem to be working, let me give you some good reasons," I said. Many of them she could not see at the time, but now she would absolutely attest to. But I gave them to her and asked her to trust me.

Here are the reasons I gave to Lillie.

1. If dating is not about marriage, why does it matter?

Remember one of the first rules we talked about? For you to grow and learn what you want, need, and don't need, you have got to view dating not as an activity to find the "one," but as an activity that produces wonderful spiritual and personal fruit. If dating is not about finding a marriage partner, *why do you care about a particular type?*

If you do care, it's a sign you have not really joined the program. You are still only looking at dating as a tool to "find the one." Otherwise, what would "type" have to do with it? It is a date, period. You can have fun talking to a "liberal," if you are conservative, or a "conservative," if you are liberal. Who cares if you don't agree with everything the person thinks and believes?

So, if you want to go out with a certain type, it may be a sign you are stuck. Give up your type. It might even be a destructive preference anyhow; at the very least, it's limiting.

2. Types are often rooted in pathology.

Wendy loved the muscular type. When I tried to get her to go out with someone who did not fit her physical template, she resisted. I pushed, and she finally agreed. Here is what happened.

When she agreed to go on a date with a guy who was not as physically "strong" as she would usually be attracted to, she did not like the experience. So, thinking that not liking something usually has some growth potential in it, I pushed her to go again. Then we talked about it.

"I liked the dates in terms of talking to him," she said. "But I felt weird. I didn't feel feminine, like I do with a strong guy."

"You mean a strong guy 'physically?'" I asked for clarification. This was a sneaky question because I knew that physical strength was not what she needed.

"Right."

"So, what is it you feel with a normal, non-Rambo type?"

"Less 'womanly.'" She had a hint of tears in her eyes.

So we talked about that feeling. More tears came.

"I have this thing about myself," she said. "I just don't feel very feminine sometimes. I wish I did, but I just don't."

We kept talking. To make a long story short, her lack of feminine feelings about herself were rooted in some feelings she had regarding years of put-downs from her brothers when she was growing up. As a result, she had gotten "hard" in her personality, or at least the shell she showed others. Underneath that shell were many tender feelings she did not allow herself to experience or share with others.

But, in her relationships with strong, macho men, who symbolized strength to her, she felt "softer," which felt good. That tender feeling made her feel more like a woman. The problem was, she was not becoming more of a woman any more than a mid-life crisis attraction to a younger person makes one twenty-two again.

Because she was trying to solve her problem through this symbol, or type, and because these macho types were not relating to the hidden, softer sides of her, she would ultimately become frustrated in the relationship. She would end it because of the macho guy's "inability" to connect. But that macho inability was part of why she chose the guy to begin with. Her "type" was part of what was keeping her stuck.

When she spent time with more balanced men, men whose strength was not just of muscles but of character, she was better able to relate from parts of herself that were hidden for so long. She learned to share and to talk from her more vulnerable sides. More of her was present and available to a typical guy.

She later fell deeply in love with a "non-specimen" man who had good character and many attractive qualities. Shortly after their marriage, she kidded with me about the amount of sexual passion they shared. It was passion that came from connection and emotional availability, not a symbolic type that always wears off.

Men do this as well. They long for physical beauty that symbolizes something to them, often to make up for something they lack. And they pick one shallow woman after another, wondering why it doesn't ever work.

Remember what I said in chapter 4, "Dating Is Not about Marriage"? There are a LOT of reasons you need to be meeting many different kinds of people, especially the ones you would not normally go out with or be attracted to. It is not only about getting the pressure off for a date to be a potential mate. It is about getting your "type" off the table as well so that you can do the following:

- Find out about all kinds of people, what they are like and what you did not know you needed.

    The young man I sent on the date with the type he would not be attracted to physically has forever changed what he looks for in a woman to take on a date. Having had the experience of being with a spiritual woman, he has really deepened in what he is looking for now, and he's finding it.

- Find out about yourself and how you need to change.

    If Wendy had not dated the non-Rambos, she would still be cut off from her feminine feelings and maybe pursuing plastic surgery to find them again. Instead, her dating experiences outside her type led her to a good man, without the surgery. And she could honestly sing the song to him, "You make me feel like a natural woman," muscles or not.

- Enjoy a good dating experience as an end in and of itself.

    Do you go to a restaurant because you are looking to buy it? Or do you go because it is a good, enjoyable experience? You can go out with someone and not fall in love with him or her. That can be a great time.

- Take the pressure off.

    Often you romantically idealize a certain type, and you are not yourself when you are around them. When you go out with those outside your type, you will be more of yourself and be able to find out more about what others are like, instead of being buried in infatuation. Plus, if your date is not the idealized type you feel you have to land, you are not clouded by your fears of rejection.

- Serve and love others.

    Learning to relate to another person in a non-self-centered way is a key relationship skill. Learn how to listen, how to get to know someone, and how to be interested in them as a human being. If you genuinely learn this, you will get out of your self-centered strivings in dating. Your ability to love will expand, and that will serve you well later in both whom you pick to fall in love with as well as how well you do with them.

- Grow in skills.

  Different types are going to pull different skills from you. If you are with an assertive person, you can practice standing up for yourself and not being dominated. If you are with an intellectual, you can practice defending your opinions and grow to think for yourself. If you are with a romantic, you can discover what you've been missing in your calculated life. If you are with a liberal and you are a conservative, or vice versa, you might learn where you have missed out on some reality. If you are with an emotionally open person, you might learn how to process and talk about feelings. If you are with an outdoor type, you might get out of your head and into the experience of God's creation and your body.

  Different types of people stretch us. We learn and grow from each other. We become more of ourselves. To stick to one type means that you might be one dimensional.

3. You don't know what you don't know.

I wish I had a list of all the times I have talked to happily married couples, and one of them has said, "Oh, he (or she) is the last person I would have thought I would end up with. He/she was not my type at all. I always went for the _____ type. But a friend of mine pressured me to go out with him, and I did. At first, I was not even open, even though we went out. But after time, I saw some things I had never known even existed. I fell more deeply in love with him than I could have ever imagined. This was so much richer and deeper. If I had not given him a chance because I was looking for my type, I shudder to think where I would be. I would certainly have missed out on the best thing of my life."

Your "type" is based on a lot of stuff inside your head, not all of it good. It is also based on ignorance of the big world of love and relationships outside your experience. This does not mean you won't end up with your type or that it is necessarily wrong. It may be the one for you.

I just talked to a man who has been happily married for twenty-five years, and he said, "She was exactly the type I had in mind from the time I was fifteen." It was really cool to see them so in love. Yet he also went out with many others who expanded his experience before he found his "type." Your type may win in the end. But make sure that it has *lots* of competition along the way! If your type wins, it ought to win fair and square.

4. Practice being a person and have good experiences.

Remember what you are doing here. You are not looking for a mate. You are practicing being a person with the opposite sex, having good experiences, and getting the numbers up—actions that can cause a lot of good things to happen. To make that happen, *you have to get past your "type."* Unless you think those FedEx uniforms are really attractive.

14

Check Your Expectations at the Door

We have talked about not limiting yourself to a specific type of person, but let's go one step further. Types are a global picture of what someone thinks he or she likes: tall, athletic, blonde, intelligent, outgoing, reserved, conservative, liberal. By definition, a type is a summary view of someone.

As I talked to Lillie and to others whose dating lives were really stuck, I found many people go much further than specifying the type of person they want. They have a laundry list of little requirements that eliminate some really good people. In fact, types, expectations, and requirements are some of the worst dynamics someone can take into dating. If you are allergic to almost all foods, finding a restaurant to have a good dinner in gets pretty difficult.

One man in his mid-thirties whom I was coaching had a real, typed-out list with a zillion requirements. On it were specific physical characteristics, such as the kind of legs she would have and the color of her hair and skin; stylistic things, such as the kind of clothes she would wear. Then he got into some pretty nitpicky spiritual things she would have to be. He went even further by specifying personal tastes in furniture, clothes, and movies. The list went on and on. I was stunned when I saw it.

Much of what he listed does not exist in the same person. They were incompatible traits! For example, he wanted someone who was not only spontaneous and creative, but also highly organized and structured. Have you ever seen those qualities in the same person?

So I went to work on him. He had himself so boxed in that I told him if he found one woman in the country who met all the expectations on that list, I would be astounded. He began to see that some things in life are important for long-term commitment and compatibility. But his expectations went way beyond those things. I laughed at many of the things he thought were so important, and I shared many stories of marriages he respected and women he respected who didn't fit his expectations. And their husbands were very much in love with them. He was amazed that people he respected had good relationships without so many of the things he had deemed "essential."

For example, among the "ideal" married women he knew, he was surprised to find they had tastes, ways of living out their faith, and even political views very different from their husbands. These differences were not at all important to their husbands; they loved their wives for who they were and for other things. This discovery rocked his categories. But he became more open.

Then it happened. He dropped some of his rigid expectations and became more open with a woman he already knew. He put their "differences" aside, which were nitpicky anyhow. He spent more time with her talking and finding out who she was. He surprised himself big time when he fell in love with her.

"I had a gem right there in front of me the whole time and could not see her," he told me. "I can't believe I was so closed." Now they are happily married.

A woman I worked with also had a big list of requirements about the status and education of the man she would date. She expected that he would be an Ivy Leaguer and that his family would come from a certain social circle. When she followed my program and threw away her list of qualifications, she met a wonderful guy who hadn't even finished college. He had gone into a service profession that he loved and for which he was acclaimed. She was surprised to find that someone who was his real self, doing what he loved, even if it was not her expectation, was very, very attractive. Her "need" for her expectation went away when she found a real person. His passion for his life and for who he was, was much more inviting than a robot with a degree.

Recently when I was speaking on dating, a man asked a question about a woman he was dating: "What do you do if you like someone but her actions don't stack up with what she says?"

"Well, that can be a serious problem," I said, thinking he referred to things such as duplicity and lying. "What is she doing?"

"Well, she says God is the most important thing in her life, but her actions don't match up with what she says. I spend an hour a day reading the Bible, and she doesn't. She wants to take the next step to get more serious, but I am reticent. If she were really serious about her relationship with God, she would study her Bible for an hour every day just as I do. I cannot get serious about her until her heart equals her actions and she starts studying her Bible like me."

"Let me ask you something," I said. "If this were the year 1204, and she said God was the most important thing to her, how would you determine if that were true?"

"What do you mean?"

"Well, if this were the year 1204, and there were no printing presses and no Bibles for everyone, and she could not study her Bible an hour every day as you do, how would you know if what she said about her relationship to God is true?"

"Probably by how she treated other people."

"And, if she talked to God, made her decisions in life based on his values, served him, and lived her life according to his principles.

In other words, maybe her expression of what spiritual commitment looks like is different from yours. What if talking to God and meditating on him is the way she connects with God, and she measured you by whether or not you went out and sat on a stump for an hour a day and talked to and thought about God? Would you measure up?"

The point was clear. He was taking *his* own definition of what commitment to God looks like and putting it on her. *His expectations were keeping him from finding out her real spirituality.* For all we know, she may have loved God a lot more than he did, but he needed to find out by getting to know her, not placing his expectations on her.

Here are some tips on both how to tell whether you have a list of expectations and on how to be more open in your dating life:

- When you meet someone, do you find yourself going down a mental "checklist"? If you do, stop that and try to get to know the person.
- When you talk to friends and others about "setting you up," do you give them a list of requirements? Do you find yourself reticent about their setting you up because the person may not meet your expectations?
- When you think about your future, do you picture yourself with a certain list of requirements for your spouse?
- Ask other people who know you well if they think you are too "picky."
- Meditate and pray on being open to meeting new people. Realize that you do not know what you need in a person and ask God to help you be humble about what you do not know.

In a later chapter, we will talk about things truly important for a long-term relationship. Some requirements, spiritual qualities, and character traits are crucial. But, remember, we are talking about dating for now, not marriage. Date with zero expectations. You might be surprised.

Forget Love at First Sight

"Love at first sight" is a myth. It should be called "brain damage" for two reasons. First, you have to have brain damage to have love at first sight, and second, if you do think what you're feeling is love, it will bring much damage to your brain as you move further along in the relationship. It is a twofold sickness. You need to be sick to get it, and when you get it, it will make you sick.

You can probably relate to love at first sight at some level, especially when you were a teenager. But in adulthood, when such feelings have the opportunity to develop into something that may be for keeps, you need to understand that there is no such thing as love at first sight.

This does not mean that there is not *something* at first sight. Nor does it mean that this something might not be very, very powerful. It can even have good elements to it. But, it is *not love*, so you should not treat it that way.

The first take-away value of this fact in dating is this: Do not let your fantasies fool you into thinking you have found something of value just because a person turns your head or makes your heart beat faster. A fast-beating heart has nothing to do with love or with anything that will last. The second take-away is this: Just because you do not fall in love at first sight does not mean that the person you meet does not have great value or even lasting potential.

Hollywood, Madison Ave., fairy tales, movies, and romance novels all add to this confusion. What used to be understood as a fantasy—something that love potions concocted by witches inflicted—is now taken as the way love itself works. It is not true, so don't believe it.

Understand that feelings such as those are based on things inside of you, not some inherent value of the person you are smitten by. What smites you is totally subjective. The reasons you feel this way about someone could be coming from a lot of sources, and sometimes it is important to find out what those are. For example, we talked earlier about Wendy, who was only attracted to men who made her feel soft and feminine. Her attraction had everything to do with her own conflicts about her vulnerability and nothing to do with the men. Ultimately, Wendy figured that out and fell in love with a non-Rambo-type guy. What if she had believed that just because someone had muscles that she was in love, only to find out later that beneath the muscles there was nothing she needed? And that she only needed the muscles because she was sick?

Here are just a few examples of real people I have worked with who have become smitten at first sight and why that feeling should not be trusted:

- The dainty woman made the man feel stronger and kept him away from his own vulnerability. When he was with her, he felt completed, connected to what he did not have in himself. As time went on, he came to resent the dainty ones he fell in love with, hating their "weakness."
- The intellectual and well-educated man made her feel so "in love." She was drawn to his pedigree and brains. Actually, this

represented getting the approval of her own prideful mother, who overvalued such things because her own upbringing did not afford them.

- The gentle man made her feel as though her prince had arrived. She was so in love with his gentle nature. Later, his lack of assertiveness and initiative drove her crazy. The gentleness she was blinded by was actually passivity, but it kept her from her fears of aggressive men, such as her father, who had hurt her.
- The successful man made her head swim. His power, accomplishments, and financial standing were so attractive to her. He seemed so strong. Actually, he was driven to succeed because he was unable to connect with anyone; he used his charm to get ahead. After the attraction wore off, he did what disconnected men do: He left her feeling alone. She was so drawn to him because she felt so powerless in the world all by herself. Latching onto him gave her a feeling of security that felt like love.
- Her "ideal" beauty drove him crazy. But when he landed her, he felt empty. She was so invested in her appearance and image, he found little to relate to. His fear of a real woman with real feelings kept him focusing on some romanticized image.

I could give you many more examples. Most of them don't end well, and the ones that do end well, it is certainly for other reasons than the fantasized love at first sight. It is because people get beyond the "love at first sight" feeling and get to know and love the real person. Love is built through soul-to-soul connection, shared values, commitment, resolving conflicts and hurts, tenderness, sacrifice, forgiveness, giving, displays of character, spiritual compatibility, and sharing—things that all have something important in common: *time*. Love takes time. Anything short of that may be exciting, even intoxicating, but it isn't love.

Enjoy your momentary rush, but realize that it has little to do with real love. Get over it and get on to the real stuff if you do continue to go out with that person. Better yet, understand this message: Real people are where the real things in life are. Go out with a lot of *real* people, not fantasies. Then you can get to know some of them and find some *real* treasures, not images of unreal things that disappear as soon as you grasp them.

16

Go Out with Almost Anyone Once, and Maybe Again

How did you two get together?" I asked Marti. She and her husband, Tony, seemed like such an amazing match.

"It was such a miracle," she said. "There is no logical way we should have ever ended up with each other."

"Why is that?"

"Well, when we met, we were in such different phases of life. I was ten years younger than Tony, and, twelve years ago, when I was twenty-four, that seemed like a big deal. I was a few years out of college, and he was a serious business guy. I would never have given him a second look for a serious relationship.

"Besides that, he seemed too 'religious' to me. I was into God and the spiritual life, but I wasn't into church at that time. I was in a season where I felt as if I had been burned by church, and I had my own thing going with God. Tony seemed to be too much like those people I was trying to get away from."

"The way that sounds, it would have taken a miracle for you to get together. How do you go from there to being married for ten years, with three kids and the picture of happiness?" I asked.

"We met at a party, and we talked for two hours. I thought he was really interesting and funny. But he was just too old, so I didn't think twice about him. It was just a conversation at a party, even though it lasted two hours!

"Then, out of the blue, he called me. I remembered him, but I thought, *Too old, too different. We'd have nothing in common.* But, I had this motto: I don't know where I got it from, maybe just because I love guys and have so many guy friends. My motto was 'go out with anybody once.' Seriously, anybody—as long as I knew they were not dangerous in some way. So, I would always know where they came from, who they were connected to, and all of that so I would not be out with the Unabomber. But other than dangerous types, I would go out with anyone.

"So I said yes. We went out, and it was awful. I think it was because I was not open to him. I had a closed mind. I did not like the date, and we really didn't connect at all. I thought that was it— a nice dinner, but on to the next one.

Then a week later he called me to go out again. To get rid of him, I said I was busy, but he asked for a different night. I said I was busy then too, so he said, 'How about tomorrow?' Literally, the door bell was ringing, 'cause I had another date with a guy who was much more my type. Since I had to go and I was not getting any-where in blowing him off, I just said okay to get off the phone.

"The next night we went out. I did *not* want to go. But he took me to dinner at one of my favorite restaurants. I think that made me be not so hard on him," she said with a laugh. "But for some reason, I opened up, and we really started to talk, and all I can say is that I *totally* connected with him. There was so much I liked about him, how he thought and the things we talked about. It was different from what I had experienced before. After that date, it was all over. We didn't get married until a couple of years later, but I knew then that he was the one for me."

Two Winning Strategies

Two good strategies to remember as you date are these: "Go out with anybody once," and "Go out with that loser again."

Going out with anyone once is closely related to the previous chapter on types. Getting rid of the mindset that there is a type for you opens you up. It clears the fog and takes off your blinders to real people, real humans you can experience and get to know. As a result, you will learn about yourself as well as the nature of relationship itself. It is about opening up your mind. This strategy is about putting that mindset to *action*.

It is one thing to have an open mind about types and to be open to other types than your own. But, if you do that, it is still possible to have other sneaky requirements, such as, "Not only is she not my type, but also I don't think I would like her." Maybe true. But you don't know. Nor do you know what you will learn. But you will never know if you don't go. So, if the person is not dangerous, if you know enough to know he is safe, why not? Why not go on a date once? You will never know until you go.

And after you go, and it was not that great, why not go again?

Here is the argument for going a second time with a date that was not very exciting. People have different parts of themselves that come out in different situations and under different conditions. Maybe the best woman you will ever meet is not a good first-impression person. Maybe she is anxious about first dates. Maybe she had a bad day with her boss and was really detached that night. Maybe she had reservations about you and was more distant than usual, as Marti was. Maybe her last boyfriend burned her, and she is skittish. You just don't know.

You can't really assume you have gotten a good picture of someone after one date. So, if you are willing to go again, you might find a very different person from the one you found during the first date. Besides that, you are just learning and experiencing anyhow, right?

(17)

Date a Non-Christian?

"What should I do?" Angela asked. "He's not a Christian, and all my Christian friends tell me I should not go out with him. But I don't get it. It's just a date. Why can't I do that?"

"I don't know why you couldn't," I said. "Why do they think that would be bad? Are you planning on marrying him that night?"

"That's what I said!" she said. "It's just a date. What are they afraid of?"

Sound familiar? If you are not a Christian, this chapter may make no sense to you, and you may ask, "What's the big deal?" But if you are, I'm sure you can identify with the above conversation. Maybe you are like Angela, who is out there dating around and thinking it would be fun to go out with someone she has met who doesn't share her faith. Nothing serious, just a date. Or, you could be one of Angela's friends, who thinks it's a really bad idea, and no matter how much fun she would have, she should avoid going on a date with a non-Christian.

What is right? Should there be a rule? What are the issues? What are the advantages?

What's the Big Deal?

Since dating sometimes leads to marriage and problems do come up when people of different faiths marry, we must explore these potential problems.

The Bible teaches that Christians should not be "yoked" with non-Christians (2 Cor. 6:14). In this section of 2 Corinthians, the apostle Paul talks about the danger of joining people who worship idols, other gods, and other ways of living, with people who worship the one true God. He tells Christians that when they follow Christ and someone they are "yoked" to does not, they have a lack of things in "common" (v. 15).

This makes sense, and it applies to most faiths if the proponents of those faiths practice them seriously. Since a person's faith directs so much of life, a couple can be torn in two different directions if they take their respective faith seriously, or if one spouse takes her faith seriously and the other one doesn't.

Deep spiritual leanings are what I call a "direction setter" in life. Unlike other differences, such as one person's interest in a hobby or taste in home décor, some differences actually pull at the direction a marriage or family takes. The desire for children is an example of a direction setter. If one person wants a child and the other one doesn't, it pulls the couple down different life paths. A vocational call can do the same thing. If one spouse wants to spend his or her life doing economic development in a Third-World country and the other wants to develop architectural designs for suburban shopping malls, they're going in different directions. These issues can divide people's time, energies, and resources.

Devout spiritual beliefs set *directions* in families. How will the kids be raised? Which values will they be taught? How will you spend holidays? How will you explain to your children why one faith is right for you and another is right for the other? What do you do when one wants to give money to their faith and you do not share that belief? Think of the tension between the husband who wants to tithe to his church and the wife who wants to spend that money remodeling the house. What about how you spend your time? Think of the family where one parent wants the Sabbath to be a day with church for everyone, while the other sees it as a time to rest, play golf, or go on family outings? What if one wants the children educated in a faith-based school and the other doesn't? These questions can pull people apart.

So Paul's advice is easy to understand. For devout Christians, the issue goes deep. One's devotion to God can be divided if one tries to keep a spouse happy who does not want him or her to be so spiritually committed. It tears the person of faith in two directions. A spouse may resent the time and attention given to God.

As a marriage counselor, I do not recommend this kind of split. Sometimes people of different faiths think that they love each other so much or are so understanding of each other that it will not be a problem. But this is rarely true; even when each person accepts the differences, each is still not sharing the most important aspect of life with their spouse. When faith cannot be shared and it is the most important thing to someone, then the heart is on a solo trip in life.

Are You Dating to Marry?

Given the potential problems, some are surprised when I say that it is sometimes fine for a Christian to go out with someone who does not share his or her faith. But, you have to remember what I have said about going out on a date: *It is not about marriage!* If you are going out just to meet people, spend time with them, get to know different types, enjoy yourself, learn about yourself and what you like and don't like, have fun experiences, share your thoughts on life, and all the things we have talked about, there is no problem. You are not going out to find someone to marry, right? At least if you are doing dating the way I have suggested.

If, however, you are a person who won't go out with an unbeliever because you will only go out with someone who could be a potential mate, then you are on an entirely different program. You are dating to marry. In my experience as a professional counselor working with singles for over twenty years, this is not the best path to take. But if that is where you are, my advice in this chapter does not apply to you.

But if you are looking to change and grow as a person in the course of dating, then accepting a date from someone with whom you do not share beliefs is a great human experience. You will learn about another person, yourself, and lots of other things. Also, if you are being yourself and not a Jekyll and Hyde (see chapter 26), then you might also have a great opportunity to share your faith with him or her; that is one of the most important things we can do. This gets us to the real issue behind all of the talk about dating someone of different beliefs than you: *Who are you?* And this issue deserves a section all to itself.

Who Are You?

The woman in the opening example of this chapter, Angela, is now happily married to an on-fire, sold-out, committed Christian. And guess what? He's the guy she referred to in her conversation with me. The unbeliever she went out with is now her committed Christian husband. What happened?

What happened was that she dated him in exactly the way we have discussed in this book. She went out with him for fun, as friends, and *with all of herself. She did not become someone else to go out with him, and when he asked to go out again, she did not turn into someone other than who she was: a committed Christian.* From the outset, she was clear about her faith. As they were going out more, she was still dating other guys. She was not getting serious about him. In fact, and here is the key: She *could not* get serious about him.

She loved God and was sold out to her faith, so she could not fall in love with someone who did not share the most important thing to her—her faith. If he did not have that, she was not going to fall for him. Why? Because of some rule? *Not really. It was because of what her heart was looking for, what her heart desired.* She desired to be with someone who could share what was in her heart, with a person of deep faith who lived it daily. If a man did not love God, she was not going to fall in love with him.

Now hear the big message here: I did *not* say that she would not *allow* herself to fall for him or would not *give herself permission* to fall in love with him. This would mean that she was capable of falling in love with someone who did not share her faith, but she would somehow be obedient to God and not go through with it, even though she would want to. This is not what I am saying.

What I am saying is that God was the most important thing to her in life; he was her very heart. So, if someone did not share that, *her heart did not have an attraction to the person* at the level where a commitment could follow. Her heart belonged to God, so she would not even want to. She was in no danger.

So, what did she do? Being a person of sold-out faith, she communicated who she was, as we will talk about in chapter 20 ("Be Yourself from the Beginning"). She shared her faith and her values. As she and her date got to be friends, she shared how she could never fall in love with someone who did not share that same faith and commitment. She said that if he wanted to go out with her, he could come to church with her or to her Bible study. She held her ground as a real person.

Long story short, he went to church with her. (As friends, remember.) She was not selling out. And he got interested. She introduced him to her community of faith, and they got to be friends with him as well. Months later, he slowly came to faith, not actually knowing when it happened. At that point, she began to see him as a person she could be potentially interested in for the long term. She watched him for a long time to see if his faith was real. They got to know each other more after that, and they slowly fell in love as they had a spiritual life to share. Now they have been married for some time and are on a track of giving themselves to service together, missions, and being models of faith in the business community where he works.

Please understand something—I am *not* giving this example as a call to missionary dating. Some people look for their "type" and can't find that person in the faith, so they think they will find their "type" outside of their faith, convert her or him, and have it all. This is not what I am saying, nor why I bring this example into the discussion.

The lesson here is that Angela was a mature Christian who was *not in danger* of falling for someone who did not share her faith. She also was a whole person from the beginning, as we said above, and she did not fudge on her faith because she liked some guy or because she was so lonely she needed him. She was grounded in a good faith community, not out there on her own. She did not become someone else to "catch" him. On the contrary, she held firm that he was going to have to come her way if he was going to spend time with her.

Also, Angela learned some things from him that she had not seen in other men. She learned that a guy could be much more complete than the ones she had dated before. He had a lot of parts that she had never found in one guy, but had dated different guys who were more one dimensional. But he liked intellectual pursuits and athletic ones. He liked the arts and the outdoors. He could be strong and sensitive. She learned that she could find men who were not so imbalanced. But, with all of this, she was always very aware that the spiritual dimension was missing.

There were things in his character that Angela really liked and that she felt she needed in someone with whom she would eventually want to spend her life. It helped her in looking at and evaluating other guys she was dating. Even if they had remained just friends, he would have been good for her. She would have learned from him.

So, if you are working the program outlined here, you are being who you truly are, and you are not spouse-shopping. In that case, I see no reason why you cannot go out with people of different spiritual persuasions. But, if you are *not* dating by the principles we have been discussing, you are in danger, and I suggest you don't date outside your faith. In fact, if the following things are true, I question whether you should even be dating.

When You Should *Not* Go Out with Someone Who Does Not Share Your Faith

- If you are looking at all of your dates as a potential mate. If this is true, you have to reread what I think about mixing faiths of people who are truly committed. So, if you are only going out with people whom you think you would marry, then you are potentially looking at a huge issue in marriage.

- If you are in danger of falling for the person. If your faith is weak and someone may become more important to you than your faith, you are in danger of having a divided heart. But, in my view, that reveals a deeper problem than dating. It says that your faith is not as important to you as Jesus says it should be. If you are a Christ-follower, then he wants all of you— your heart, mind, soul, and strength. If many parts of your heart don't really belong to God, that's the real problem. Would you go for someone who did not want to pursue your spiritual life with you? Is God not your highest desire? Take a look and talk to the ones who help you spiritually to find out why that is true.

- If you are lonely. Lonely people are especially vulnerable to anyone who wants to be with them. If this is the case, you should not be dating seriously at all, for it puts you in danger of getting involved with someone to cure the loneliness. Get help for that and get plugged into a community first.

- If you are on a solo spiritual trip. If you are a Christian, your faith dictates that you are in spiritual community with others who are nurturing your faith. If you are not, you are spiritually vulnerable to not having the input that keeps you on track with your faith and values. Do not go it alone. Stay in community, and if you are not, fix that first and then worry about dating. You need them anyway. (See chapter 11 on "Get Your Team Together.")

- If you are sexually impulsive. Let's be honest here. If you do not have self-control and you are going out with someone whose values and morals permit sex outside of marriage, you are vulnerable. So, don't think about it. Get with your spiritual community and work this out.

Months ago, I had dinner with a friend who lived out the opposite of what Angela did. He began dating a very nice woman who did not share his faith, so he unplugged from his spiritual community. She was a lovely person, and he found himself desiring more with her. But he did *not* share his faith with her. In fact, when it became clear that she was not interested in his faith, he all but quit talking about it. He put God on the shelf. He went her way, to an interesting, secular life. They enjoyed fun times and built a relationship, leaving faith out of it.

Concerned about him, his Christian friends encouraged him to be more honest with her about what was important to him. They were concerned for her as well, as he was not being honest about who he was. He did not take their advice. He kept seeing her. Then, they moved in together. A few months later, he was considering marriage.

But, before he proposed, he came to see me and poured out his heart. What he said was sad but real. "I am miserable," he told me. "She is a wonderful girl, and I love so much about her. But it is tearing me up that I cannot share my spiritual life with her. I just can't go through with this, but I am too far into it now. What do I do? I can't be happy, divided inside like this."

It was a sad dinner. I asked him if he wanted to feel the way he did right then for the rest of his life. Did he want to continue to lie to her and be unfair to her as well? He had not been clear with her. That was not right. If they got married, he would slowly come out with all of this spiritual stuff, and she would feel deceived. That is certainly not treating someone as you would want to be treated.

He had to make a tough call and be honest with her. The relationship ended soon thereafter. Recently we had dinner again, and he recounted the whole affair. He swore to himself that he would never go through that again. But he understood that the problem was not just that he had gotten too involved with someone who did not share his faith. *The real problem was that he had not gotten involved enough in his own faith, and he had not lived that out and been clear from the beginning.*

He traced the problem back to getting out of his spiritual community and being too focused on finding "the one." His idol was marriage. When he had turned thirty-four, he felt as if he was getting too "old" to not be married, and he really needed to find someone. That is really young to hit the panic button. This lesson is really about all the rules we have talked about. Don't get obsessed with finding a mate; be yourself, get your spiritual act together, be healthy, stay plugged into your team, and so on. If you are doing all these things, then go out with whomever you want. If you are not, then be very careful, no matter what faith you profess.

Drop Your Hankie (or Palm Pilot)

My friend Stacy and her friend Gretchen recently went to a party where there were a lot of single men. Stacy is married, and Gretchen is not. The whole drive there, Gretchen filled Stacy's ear with her disappointment in her dating life. She complained about everything from "there are no good men out there" to "all they are interested in is some 'model.'" By the time they got to the party, Stacy felt sad for her friend.

When they got there, they hung out together and talked to a lot of people, catching up on old friends and having a good time. As time went on, Stacy noticed something. All the single men at the event were milling around the room talking to various women, including herself. She found them delightful: "They were so cute," she said to me later. "I wished I could be back dating! Not really, but I do miss it, meeting guys and all of that. It is just so much fun.

"But here is my problem. I don't know what to say to Gretchen. I know what is wrong. It is *not* that there are no cute guys around, or good ones. I met several tonight. But I watched her, and although she is not rude or anything, she is just not very open or inviting. Whenever a man looked at her, she looked away. If I were a guy, I would think she wasn't interested. What do I tell her? I want to say, 'If you are interested in getting a date, tell your face!' She is just not coming across as if she wants to meet anyone.

"How can I tell her to lighten up and learn how to flirt?" she added. "Isn't that just a part of being a woman? Doesn't God just wire that into you somewhere? How can I get her to open up?"

What do you think? Is flirting part of a woman's "wiring?" What is it, exactly? Do men do it? How does a man show a woman he's interested in meeting her? The world abounds with theories, rules, and prohibitions about how women and men meet. But it's not that complicated.

Here is how people normally get together. A man notices a woman, and the woman notices him back, or notices him noticing her. At that moment, something is going to happen. The phone is ringing and you answer it, or you play a "You have reached a number that has been disconnected" message, or you give a busy signal. If you want to be talked to in a group, like church or a party or some other gathering where singles are, you have to show you are open to being talked to. The easiest way? Look the person in the eye and if you want to, smile. Just look at them, and they will know. People who are not open to meeting others usually avoid eye contact. Open people make a lot of eye contact. This is not rocket science. Go to a preschool and watch kids who want to play with someone. They just go up to another child and say, "Hi, want to play?" You can learn from them.

Once that happens, in my belief, it is the natural order for one person to notice the other, and the other to notice them back. If an individual sees someone who is friendly or open, he or she will go up and say "Hi" or introduce himself or herself. At that point, they can have a normal conversation and interact like social creatures. The rest should follow. But that usually won't happen if he has looked at her and she doesn't make eye contact, or if she somehow gives a signal that she is closed off as a person. Many men won't take the next step toward what they perceive as a closed door. (Although I think they should; see chapter 22, "Where Is the Testosterone?") Also, it is sometimes helpful for a woman to find a way to approach a man and strike up a conversation. Many men love being approached by a friendly woman to socialize. It takes a lot of the wondering and pressure off of them. So, women, be nice!

Here are some things you can do. Introduce yourself, go say hi, and ask if he is new to the group or the company. Make him feel welcome. If not, find out how long he has been coming there. Ask questions, such as, "So, how did you end up here?"

This is not brain surgery. But it is amazing how many women are stuck, who do not interact. In chapter 24 I will share a story about some women at a bachelorette party that illustrates how good opportunities can be lost by women not being open. One woman there, who had worked the program outlined in this book and was now married, remarked, "I was the only one making eye contact because I am so used to it, but I had to keep looking back down because I am married." She described how two men had approached their table *twice* to meet them, but she lamented that *"all the girls were so NOT to the point of being open. They were just clueless and missed an opportunity."*

So think about your own actions and ask the others who know you: "If you saw me at a party or at church, would you approach me?" Get some feedback. Have them watch you at an event. You might be surprised that just because you want people to interact with you doesn't mean you are giving off that signal. Find out if you appear closed, shut down, or not "approachable."

Think about moving out of your normal comfort zone. Go talk to someone. Say hello and ask some questions. Meet that person and introduce yourself. This does not have to seem like a "come on." This is simply how people meet. If you ask couples how they met, you will find that many of them were at the same place *but not together*, and one of them introduced himself or herself to the other. You have to meet somehow, and if there is no one there to do it for you, it is up to you. Besides, meeting people is fun. Go for it, and remember, look them in the eye!

I know we are in the twenty-first century, but whatever happened to dropping the hankie? Try some version of dropping your hankie, and someone you like may return it to you (or guys, your Palm Pilot). Those phrases, including Cinderella's slipper, came from somewhere because they have truth to them. And remember, smile!

Follow a Strategy from Beginning to Middle to End

▮ ▮

Tom had just gotten out of his one millionth failed dating rela-tionship. He was good at finding dates, but he was unsuccessful at making a relationship work for very long. He was a "serial monog-amous" dater. He would find a woman he liked and stop going out with all others. He would lock in on one woman too quickly.

There is nothing wrong with finding someone you like and stop-ping the dating of others. This normally happens when you find someone who might be a good candidate for marriage. However, far too many people do not find the right person to get more serious with *in the context of going out with enough other people.* Such people break up with one exclusive individual, and they don't date many others before finding the next exclusive relationship. Going out with lots of people would help them to know what they want and to evaluate what they have found. Certainly you can't be serious with someone and continue dating everyone else. But you can be dating a lot of people in general. And *then*, when there is one of those you really like, you can get more serious. My point is that people break up with one exclusive one, and don't date that many people before finding the next one they get exclusive with.

Getting more serious is something that happens when someone "stands out" among the crowd. "There is something different about this one," you hear relationally successful people say. At that point, the others fade into the background. But it's too easy for someone to "stand out" if he or she is the only one standing!

So, what I said to Tom was that I wanted him to follow a rule. When he came to me for advice, I made him promise to go out with at least five women at the same time instead of getting serious with one. By "going out," I didn't mean getting serious—that is, going out with one woman zillions of times, implying that he was interested when he was not or that there were no others in the picture. I was not advocating any duplicity hurtful to a woman. I wanted Tom to go out on many casual, friendly dates and to tell those women he dated that he was not looking to get serious or exclusive with anyone at this juncture in his life. He was having fun, and if that was cool with someone, it was cool. If they wanted more, tell them he was the wrong guy. Just don't go from meeting someone to being exclusive with someone with little in between.

Unfortunately, Tom did not follow my advice. He started to, but then he quickly attached himself to another woman, and he went down the same road again. My hope is that he will "get it" at his two millionth relationship, when his dating life is still not working. My point in asking Tom to date many women was this:

Tom needed to follow a dating strategy through from beginning to middle to end.

Healthy dating follows a three-phase process—from beginning to middle to end—and each phase has a unique strategy. Tom had just one strategy: Find one you are interested in, move in, get serious, get exclusive, and get married. That's a strategy all right—a strategy for disaster.

Dating has different phases, and each phase has different strategies. For example, in phase one, don't go on a first date with an eye toward the altar. Your own phases and strategy may be different from someone else's, depending on your history and experience, but *there should be a process from dating casually to making a more significant commitment.* Below is what I mean by different phases with different tasks at each phase.

Phase One: Fun

In phase one you have no interest and no attachment to anyone special. You don't even have any expectations or a list, as we have discussed earlier. You are open, and you are dating. You're going out and having fun; you're getting to know and observe people. You're experiencing other human beings.

Your strategy for this phase is just that—to have fun and to experience. There are three main things you should experience.

1. The person. You are dating, in part, to learn about people, remember? So, observe the people you date. Here are some questions you can review before and answer after you go on a date:

- What appealing qualities does this person have?
- What unappealing qualities does this person have?
- What spiritual qualities does this person have? How are these qualities similar to or different from your own?
- What characteristics do you see in this person that would characterize someone with whom you could get serious?
- What characteristics do you see in this person you definitely do not want to see in someone with whom you get serious?
- How do those qualities and characteristics affect you—positively and negatively?

- Do you notice anything surprising about this person or yourself? If so, what is it?
- How are you being stretched? What things might you have thought negatively about before but now, upon closer inspection, look different?
- What did you learn about this person's activities, interests, and life passions?
- Does this person remind you of any significant person in your life? Is that positive or negative?

In other words, this first phase should be fun, stretching, and insightful. Did you notice anything in that list about "how do I get this person to like or marry me?" Just reminding you.

2. Yourself. Here are some questions to help you monitor yourself when you are dating:

- What are your reactions to the person? Do you find yourself attracted? Why? Is it sick or healthy?
- Are you romantically idealizing this person? (If you are ready to sell everything and move away with this person, go to chapter 12, "Tie Me to a Tree.") Analyze why you are so instantly smitten.
- Do you overvalue appearance? Style? Some other characteristic?
- Do you find yourself not attracted? Why? Is that a good thing or a bad thing?
- Are you turned off because this person seems stable and "boring"? Compare that to your last relationship with someone whose life was characterized by chaos and risk taking when what you really longed for was someone whose life was stable. Now that you are looking at it, how does it seem? Is that good or bad?
- What things about the person do you find are making you feel or think differently than you thought you might? Why?
- What parts of you do you experience when with this person? Is that new? What does that say to you? Have you felt this way before? Is there a pattern?

- What are your fears and insecurities with this person? What is your strange behavior? How are you not yourself?
- If they remind you of someone significant, is that good or bad? Have you not healed from someone significant in your history?
- Do you open up or shut down around certain traits this person has? (One man, for example, said he felt himself come alive when the woman he dated made a decision about where to go for dinner. He started to like her. But this meant something bad for him. He had a history of being passive with strong women whom he ultimately felt controlled by, like his mother.) Watch your reactions and learn from them.

In other words, this is a time to see what you feel, think, and fear. Get off your autopilot and become aware of yourself (see chapter 30, "Turn off the Autopilot and Drive"). What does your experience with this person tell you about the only one you can do anything about: *you*?

3. The experiences themselves. Dating is a great time to learn about life and various activities. Whatever you are doing, take it in! Museums, dining, movies, church, retreats, sports, libraries, parties—all have meaning for you.

- Does an activity awaken a part of you that has been asleep? Many times people discover new things they love through dating.
- What were you doing together when you felt something "strong"? "Intense"? "Repulsive"? "Scary"? What does that say about you? What role does that particular activity play in your history (e.g., romance, intimacy, sexuality, arguing, disagreeing, having fun, spirituality, and so on)?
- What is familiar or unfamiliar about the experience? Is it a "stretching" one, or an old one you would do better to leave behind?
- If this experience is a big part of you or the other person, is there a match? If not, and you had to do or not do a lot of

this activity as a result of being in a relationship with this person, how would that feel?

Use this time to grow in life and as a person. Take the growth experiences and let them stretch and teach you about life and become a better person, emotionally, physically, intellectually, and spiritually.

Phase Two: Interest

If you continue to go out, this person has sparked some interest in you. This may mean interest for a long-term relationship, or it may not. Maybe you want to continue to date the person without thought to the long term. Many friendships/casual dating relationships are meaningful for both people but were never intended to go the distance. They are fun, often healing, spiritually enriching, and meaningful in many other ways. The people learn from each other.

Sometimes, though, something about the person has sparked your interest, and that something may be more than just a desire to have more fun and experiences with this person as a friend. You see something to which you might be really attracted, and you think this has long-term potential.

But even if that is the case, remember, *you are still just learning about them.* So, keep going out with others as well. Don't be exclusive. There is no reason to be, remember? Just because you are attracted to someone does not mean you give up all boundaries and fold the deck, as Tom did. Keep looking around, experiencing other people and things. Doing this will keep you from getting swept up in idealization and fusion (the desire to glue yourselves together), and it will also keep you looking at others and realizing that this is not the only fish in the sea.

Some internal things may be happening that you need to look at. If you continue to date someone, the possibility for growth, attachment, fear, dysfunction, sexual awakenings, and spiritual growth, and all sorts of other things begin to increase. It is *very* important for you to process all of this with your team. Get feedback on the person and on yourself.

What are the patterns you find yourself living out? Are they old? Are they dysfunctional? Are they the same ones you followed before on autopilot, and you know where they lead? It's time to act differently before you end up where you have before. It's time to learn new patterns that you have not tried before as your coaches help you. Continue to learn and do not give away your heart or the farm. You can't get a prenuptial on your heart and soul. If you are in this phase of getting to know someone, hold on to your heart. Notice who the person is; look at his or her behavior and character. Observe and learn.

This is not a time to surrender your separateness or give up your boundaries. Keep the dating casual, not as though you were a "couple." Remember, other people are still in the picture. Avoid the coupling thing, whatever that looks like for you, in this phase. If the other person likes you, that person's respect for you and interest in you will increase if you have a life apart from him or her.

Don't begin merging your lives in symbolic ways. Maintaining your separateness is an attractive quality. If you give up all boundaries at this point, it will communicate too much interest, lack of limits, dependency, and hunger that don't belong in this second phase. Avoid too much availability, too many spontaneous get-togethers, too many last-minute dates, which would indicate you have nothing in your life other than this person.

If you feel yourself getting more interested, ask yourself why. Is it a healthy attraction? Is it for one of the bad reasons we list in chapter 26, "Don't Be Dr. Jekyll or Mr. Hyde"? If so, let that be a big warning and a sign to spend time doing some hard work on your head.

If it is turning into more interest for good reasons, as best you can tell, then you are moving into Phase Three.

Phase Three: A Closer Look

This is the phase where you know you have more interest in this person than just someone you go out with for fun. You want to get to know more about him or her, and you think the relationship could really go somewhere. You are becoming more open and maybe even more vulnerable. There seems to be a little special-ness. So, what now?

First of all, if your heart is waking up to this person, ask yourself the hard questions, with your team. Why are you getting into this person? Are these good reasons? If your heart is getting involved, you had better be looking below the surface. If you are attracted to this person because of charm, physical attraction, sexual or romantic chemistry, talents, intellect, status, achievement, outside appearance of spirituality . . . great, those are all fun. But,

those things have nothing to do with the success of a relationship.

Many criminals have all of these traits. If you think you could fall in love with and get serious about this person, *look harder at character*. I hope you have been noticing character all along, but if your heart is getting involved, really put on the glasses. We will go into the specifics of character in chapter 32 on "Beauty Is Only Skin Deep but Character Goes All the Way to the Bone," but let me just say here that this is time for you to look at the real person, behind all the things that have drawn you in.

It is time to take a much harder look at things like morals, real spiritual maturity (not external religious talk), relational abilities, emotional and psychological maturity, work and career history and plans, personal habits, passions and aspirations, and other stuff that if you did get serious, you would end up experiencing a lot more than a person's "good looks." *Character is not only important. It is most important.*

By now you are spending enough time with the person to see if values are really backed up by behavior. You can see if the walk matches the talk. You can see more of how the person really is in relationship. And this look at character and relationship realities becomes the determining factor in whether or not you go to the next levels, which are more serious and which sometimes lead to commitment and marriage.

Not All or Nothing

This is all really common sense. *But it is amazing how many people throw common sense out the window when it comes to dating and marriage.* You would never invite a stranger off the street into your house and give him or her the keys and full access to all you own. But in matters of the heart, people do that every day. With little or no background checks, they give away their hearts, souls, and very lives. Because it is "love," it seems to fall under different rules. "If it feels so good, it has to be right." Nothing is further from the truth. Things can feel very good, and be oh-so-bad.

The best defenses against this happening are your own character, spiritual maturity, relational maturity, time, wisdom, trusted friends to give you wise counsel, prayer, faithfulness to your spiritual commitments, and structuring the dating process into its proper phases. Don't go from nothing with a person to giving him or her all of you without the proper process. Basic due diligence is required, but it takes longer than your hormones or fantasies may want it to.

Go one phase at a time, and don't rush it! If it is good, real, and true, it will make it through all the phases. This is the only way good fruit is ever produced, by going through all the phases of growth. You can't have a good tree in a minute. But if you grow it the right way, including taking time, then you will know the true character of the person you are with. As David wrote:

> *They are like trees planted along the riverbank,*
> *bearing fruit each season without fail.*
> *(Psalm 1:3, NLT)*

Give the person time, and give each phase its time as well. It will pay off in the bad relationships you avoid—and the good one you find.

Be Yourself from the Beginning

Okay, how many of you women would go out on a first date with someone and let him see you like you would let him see you after six months of dating? Or like you look when you are just hanging out at home, not expecting anyone to drop by—no makeup, sweats, undone hair?" I asked the crowd. "And how many of you men would go out on a first date in a ratty old T-shirt with no shower?"

"No way!" came the unanimous response, along with nervous laughter and comments. There was no way the women were going to be caught looking less than their best. At the beginning of a relationship, women wear makeup, dress their best, and fix their hair in an attractive style, and men take a shower and put on a clean shirt. Everyone wants to make a good first impression.

First impressions, or early impressions, are important. They give you the opportunity to make second and third impressions. Blow it too badly on the first date, and there may not be a second one. So, there is nothing wrong with trying to look good or impress your date. That is part of the game. But, *making a **good** impression and making a **false** impression are two different things.*

Certainly you don't want to scare someone off by displaying your worst side. But this rule, "Be yourself from the beginning," means that, in trying to impress someone, you should not become someone you are not just to get him or her to like you better. You will encounter several problems if you do.

1. A person who just complies with the other person's opinions and wishes displays very little attractiveness or energy.

If you are trying to get someone to like you by not disagreeing with him, or acting as though you like everything he does, or "molding" to who he is, you might as well kiss love goodbye. If he is attracted to your "non-person" way of being with him, you are most likely with a very self-centered person who only enjoys someone who mirrors everything he thinks or likes. Over time he will get bored with such an adaptive person. To the degree you are a mirror, you are disposable.

Healthy attraction is fueled by desire for a real person, a person who is separate from the other and who has her own feelings, opinions, and tastes. That sense of "you are not me" fuels attraction. Space creates longing. The best way to have someone get bored with you is to be whatever that person wants. Healthy romantic energy and a person's individuality are intertwined. This is why the "pursuit" is sometimes such a "charged" time. The separateness and inability to possess the other person is greatest then.

In a good relationship, that sense of charged separateness continues even after someone is "caught." To foster that, you have to make sure you continue to be an individual throughout your relationship. Even when you are like the other person, when you are real, your realness has energy. So, alike or different, be real.

2. Being accepted, when false, is worse.

Your date's accepting you when you are not being yourself is even worse. If she is not the type who wants a mirror, she might be the controlling type who just wants her own way. She does not have to deal with a real person who does not always do what she wants. This is not love, and you will experience no intimacy going forward, as you are not truly known.

Also, when you do tire of not being yourself and you show who you really are and the things that are important to you, she will cry "Foul," and great conflict will follow. Sometimes, sadly, this kind of "getting real" comes after marriage and often results in divorce. This would never happen if from day one you are just yourself.

3. If you are not genuine, you are less likely to attract a genuine person.

Later, we will take a closer look at the role of the lack of genuineness, or duplicity, in dating. It causes unhealthy attractions and also attracts the wrong type. But I list it here because being who you are from the beginning prevents duplicitous connections. Genuine attracts genuine, as whole attracts whole. Fake attracts fake, as duplicity attracts duplicity.

4. If you are not yourself, you give the person less to be attracted to.

We talked about how separateness creates romantic energy and fuels healthy attraction. In addition to the separateness that being yourself creates, more of you shows up in the relationship as well. There are more parts of you to be seen if you do not hide them. While you may not realize the attractiveness of different little parts of who you are, those qualities might be very attractive to someone else.

"I love it that he liked independent films," a friend said. "I thought that was so different and unique." Do you think he knew that some random taste he had would be attractive to her? He didn't. But if he had not shown what he really liked and just did everything her way, she would not have seen that part of him.

Trying to like what the other person likes or to be what they want you to be hides many things about you that could be very attractive to a good person.

Dating is about finding out who you are and who others are. If you show up in a masquerade outfit, neither is going to happen. I cannot overemphasize the absolute importance of being yourself. It will dictate whom you attract, whom you are attracted to, what happens later, and whether or not it will last. Being yourself is life or death for love.

If you like physical exercise, say it and show it. If you don't, be honest about it. Then the other person might introduce you to it, and it will be a growth step for your relationship.

If you don't like certain kinds of foods, say it. Speak up. Then you can go her way to restaurants whose food you don't care for as a gift and sacrifice, and she will appreciate your flexibility: "I don't usually like it, but I'll try it." What a nice person, she thinks. You might even learn you like it! Either way, you win. She feels as though you gave her something by eating Indian food, but you remained a well-defined person.

If you don't want to go to a certain movie, say it. You could also say, "I'll give it a try if you really want to, but it isn't the kind of movie I usually like. Let's trade. I'll go see this suspense thriller, if you'll go with me to see the foreign film!" You are still being who you are, even when you are giving to him.

You could remain silent and just deny yourself, which is a good and important quality for relationships, but that will only work if you are being real in other areas. Self-denial runs shallow if a person is totally adaptive everywhere. Don't make a big issue or statement about every decision or conversation. What a pill you would be! Go the other person's way at times too without making a big issue. But, in the whole of things, be yourself. That is what is important.

The list could go on and on. I just coached a couple who could not have been more different in many of their tastes when they began dating. But they were honest about it, and it created great chemistry. They both learned a lot, and both grew. Now they are married and enjoying each other's differences. If they had not been clear about them, it may have been a different story.

Not being yourself may be the reason none of your relationships so far have worked. You might be like Julia Roberts in the movie *Runaway Bride*. Julia Roberts' character, Maggie Carpenter, flees her grooms at the last possible minute. Her several failed relationships may have been caused by her inability to be herself. In one scene, all of her past fiancés were asked what kind of eggs Maggie liked, and each one of them said she liked her eggs fixed as he did. The problem was they all liked their eggs fixed in different ways. She had become whatever she thought the guy liked. Small wonder she was never able to find love. In one scene, Richard Gere, who plays New York columnist Ike Graham, confronts her for conforming to all her boyfriends.

She calls her conformity being "supportive."

"Supportive?" he replies. "You weren't being supportive. You were being scared. Just like now. You are the most lost woman I have ever laid eyes on."

"Lost!"

"That's right. You're so lost, you don't even know how you like your eggs."

She got the message. Beginning with something as small as an egg, she began to express who she really was. The result? The good guy fell in love with her, and she was finally in love for the first time.

Remember, dating and even resulting love are about truly getting to know another person—the real one. If you are going to go on a date, go. Show up, with the real you.

- If you are looking for a real person, remember something: Be one. Here are some tips: Try to stay in touch with your own thoughts and opinions as well as those of your date, and don't ignore what you think and feel just because the other person is different.
- Watch how you hide who you really are. When do you do that? What were you afraid of?
- After your date, talk to your team about what you did. Ask them to explore with you why you acted that way.
- Review your past dating relationships and look at your tendencies to not be yourself and the problems it caused. List examples of when you did that and the result. Talk it over with a friend.
- Ask that same friend to help you in your present dating to not do that again. Ask him or her to hold you accountable.

- Are there specific areas where you tend to not be yourself? Are there certain areas (opinions, tastes, thoughts and views, dislikes, boundaries, sex, spirituality, politics, hobbies) where you feel more pressure to conform or give yourself away? Discover what those are and ask your team to help you to change.
- Are you "yourself" in appearance? Do you hide your body? Do you feel pressure to hide your real appearance or to look like someone else?

Remember, when you go out on a date, make sure you go! If you do, you might find what you are looking for.

21

Don't Play Games

I'm going to see Ryan again tonight," Lisa told her friend Samantha. "What! Don't do that. Don't you know that if you go out with him again so soon you are sending him a message that you are easy, and he won't appreciate you because he won't have the thrill of a chase? Didn't you read *The Rules*?" Samantha exclaimed.

"Oh, really? Gosh, I don't want to send him the wrong message. What should I do? What if I call him and tell him I have a big proposal due at work and can't go? How is that?"

"No, I don't think so," Samantha coached. "That would not help because he already knows you would have gone if you didn't have work to do. You have to do something different now that you are in it. Just go, but be distant. Don't act so eager, the way you sound with me. He will think you are not that interested, and then he will try harder."

"What if he tries to hold my hand or kiss me goodnight or something? Do I let him?"

"No, don't do that. Don't even get into the situation at the door. End the date a little early. Tell him you are tired and have an early meeting, thank him, and then just go to your door. Shake his hand or something. Just keep him guessing."

"But he was so nice and real last night. What if he just wants to talk more or something? I don't want to make him feel rejected."

"Never give him more time than the date. It is a power imbalance. Keep the upper hand, and he will find you more attractive."

"But I don't want power. I just want to get to know him. And he wants to get to know me. What's so bad about a cup of tea?"

"Fine. But don't come crying to me when he doesn't call you any more after tonight."

Now Lisa was worried, and she was not looking forward to her date as she had been. She didn't even know what to wear. This dating thing was too complicated. It seemed a lot like warfare to her.

Meanwhile, Ryan was talking to a friend of his.

"What are you doing tonight?" Justin asked.

"I have a date with that new girl I told you about."

"Oh, yeah? Didn't you go out with her last night?"

"Yeah, it was great. She seemed so much more normal than a lot of women I know and without all the game-playing. Just real. We had a good time, and I had these tickets for tonight, so I said, 'What the heck?' and just asked her. Turned out she was free, and we are going. I really liked her spontaneity and willingness to make a decision on the spur of the moment. Spontaneity is a big deal to me. So is being confident enough to not play all those dating games—playing hard to get and all of that stuff. She seemed like she had a good time and showed it by agreeing to go out again. I really like that. Seems like she is pretty secure in herself."

"Cool, wish I could find one like that . . ." Justin said.

So Ryan is now looking forward to going out with the open, genuine, real, connecting woman he went out with the night before, and he is about to meet a chess game with a wall of armor. Is that going to help? Further, Lisa will be a nervous wreck, wondering what "kill the deal" decisions she may be making if she orders the wrong kind of salad.

"These foolish games are tearing me apart," is more than a line from a pop song. Many people wonder about whether they need to play games in dating. What should you do or not do when you date? What is helpful? What is not?

The Issues behind Game-Playing

Depending on whom you talk to, you'll hear many strategies on dating, many of them contradictory. Some say flatter her; others say withhold compliments so she doesn't get a big head. Some say make yourself available or he will find someone who is; others say he only appreciates someone he has to chase. And on and on. What is true?

Actually, these "games" have been designed to deal with some important issues, but there is a better way to handle these issues than driving yourself crazy trying to figure out every move in the dating game. If you understand what's behind all the strategies and if you deal with these matters naturally, you won't have to worry. To the pure, all things are pure. What are the issues? Let's look at them.

Available vs. Hard to Get

There is truth to the idea that we appreciate things that don't come too easily, but at the same time, things have to be achievable. Good restaurants generally require a reservation; you just cannot walk in. Why? Because they don't allow it? No, that's not why. *Rather, because they have a lot of other people who want a table.* So you have to make sure you call ahead. But if you call, and you can't get a reservation for six months, you lose interest. It's too much of a hassle to try to go there.

The reason we appreciate things that don't come too easily is not only because we have to work for them, but also because these things truly have value. Working for something in and of itself is not what gives it value. If you had to work for four years for a candy bar, you would not do it, but you might work that long for a medical degree. The willingness to work arises from the value of the desired object. The work alone does not make the object desirable.

What does this mean for dating? You should not be so without a life, so needy, and so desperate that *you are always able to seat someone at your table*. The person with a full life is attractive because she has interests beyond whoever is asking her out. She may not necessarily have a lot of dates every night, but she has a book group, a prayer group, or friends with whom she has planned to go out to dinner or go to a movie. Or, imagine this: "No, I can't go out tomorrow because I'm reading a good book and I'm really looking forward to some time alone to do that. How about another night?"

This is not playing hard to get. It's being real about the life you have. And here is the kicker—this message comes across. As I said above, "To the pure, all things are pure." The person who has a full life sometimes *did* have a really good time and *does* happen to be available the next night, as Lisa was. And spontaneity can be good. So, she says, "Let's go for it," and does something on a whim. But the deeper reality—that she is a solid person whose life is full without this date—is communicated. Ryan knows she is a full-life person. And the date is just a date.

If being real and available turns someone off, then he might be the kind of person you don't want anyhow. He might be the kind who only wants what he can't have and who is only into the chase. You don't want a person who only wants the unattainable. He won't appreciate what he is actually able to have until he works through whatever is driving that motivation. Let him do that somewhere else with someone else.

One man told me that in the third week of dating the woman who is now his wife, she called around nine one night and said, "I just got out of the movies. What are you doing?" He was at home watching TV and told her to come by. They had a wonderful time; he saw a whole new side of her and loved that she was real enough to just call him up at the spur of the moment and drop by. "She was different from other women who called all the time and were too available. She had a life, and I knew that when she did call, it was more natural. It made me open up."

Be yourself, be real, and have a full life, and that will come through.

Living Your Life vs. Jettisoning it for Your Date

Don't adapt your life to the other person too much or too soon. While you might not have an empty life, as soon as someone you like comes along, you empty yourself of the life you have. This sends the message that you are so needy for a relationship that you will throw everything else out the window for this person. You give off a very real unconscious vibe when you do that. The power imbalance is not only real, but also sick. It says that the person has too much power in your life. You need him too much. And no one wants to be in a relationship with a parasite.

This is why some people think playing games is helpful. They really do want to suck this person into the vacuum in their life, but they are strategic and say no to the date tomorrow to act as if they are not parasites; however, all they do is hold the parasite in themselves at bay. They go out next week, and they are the same parasite, just a week later. Their date is *still going to get the vibe*. The game is not going to cure their dependency.

So, even if you have a life, if you have such a need for the relationship that you would instantly get rid of your other commitments because you have to have this person, let that be a signal. Keep your other things going, and work the date into your life. Don't keep your life at bay so that the person will immediately have all your time. Find out what that dependency and willingness to abandon it all are about. Get plugged in to some support or help for that loneliness or whatever else is driving that hunger. If you have a vacuum, your date will pick up on it no matter what your strategy.

Some women do not buy a house because they are planning on finding a husband and getting married. They do not want to appear as though they are too independent and are planning on being single for the rest of their life. Dumb reason for not buying a house. If you want a house, get it. Have a life. Don't worry; if you find the right guy, he will appreciate your independence, and selling a house is what realtors are for.

Respect vs. No Boundaries

Another dynamic that games cover up is a lack of self-respect, other-respect, or boundaries. Most of the suggestions you hear people making, such as "Don't accept a Saturday-night date after Wednesday," or "Don't see him more than once or twice a week," are really designed to communicate that you have good boundaries, self-respect, and respect for the other person. These are huge issues.

For self-respect reasons, you should not be too available. Self-respect comes through when you do not allow someone to treat you as something less than a person with your own time, feelings, needs, and desires. Proper respect for someone's time and life does not allow for lots of last-minute-only dates.

For someone who *always* calls at the last minute, make your plans, and then when he calls, show self-respect. "I would love to, but I have plans. Usually I need a little notice for weekends. They get pretty busy. Give me some notice next time, and I'd love to go."

Being late, not calling when he said he would, and not following through are sure signs of nonrespect. If you are running into behavior where someone feels as though he can have you or treat you any way he wants without being respectful of your feelings, say no to that. For someone who shows up very late for a date without a call, don't be a snit about it. Just tell him you understand getting caught at work, but say, "Let me know if you are going to be that late, and I will be able to use the time."

You should know in your gut if you are being pursued and desired, or being used and taken for granted. Lisa was being desired and pursued. Ryan had enjoyed being with her and had tickets to a game that night. It was a great idea. But, if that is how Ryan operated all the time, Lisa would feel taken for granted. And she should let him know she has a life and she needs him to plan ahead. If he wants to go out, he has to let her know before the "day of." Command common respect.

I Say I Like You vs. I Keep You Guessing

Another dynamic that can get gamey is whether or not someone who likes another person lets him or her know. Again, this whole thing revolves around some underlying issues: idealization and flattery on the one hand, and withholding affection and being unattainable on the other.

In the first instance, a woman (who has something lacking inside) meets a man. She is looking for an ideal prince to make her life better. She has a fantasy. When someone who symbolizes that fantasy comes along, he blows her away. She loses it. He is beyond her dreams. He is incredible. She can't sleep, or eat, or work. She thinks everything he does is so cute or worthy of worship that she flatters him right from the beginning.

I remember one guy telling me, "On the second date, she said, 'You are the most amazing man I have ever met.' *I could not get out of there fast enough.* I could tell she was into some fantasy about me I wanted no part of. And I had thought she was really cool until she said that."

And guys do the same thing with women. From the beginning they idealize the woman they are dating, and the power shifts. Not that the game is to hold onto power, but an imbalance of power can be unhealthy. People who idealize other people operate out of a vacuum, and that vacuum shows up sooner or later, usually sooner. The idealized one, if she is healthy, runs or finds herself suddenly losing interest. "Get me out of here," her heart says, often not even knowing why.

The other side of a power imbalance occurs when people withhold compliments or affection from the other person. They feel threatened, so they withhold showing their "like." They think that withholding their "like" of the other person is going to give them more power in the relationship. But again, *the problem is not in the strategy but in the underlying issue*—the threat they feel because of a vacuum inside of them. They don't feel lovable, so they have to fuse with someone they idealize to make up for it, or they have to hide their attraction to show they are not empty in some way. Either strategy reveals a deeper problem.

Healthy people do neither. They do not idealize a person, nor do they withhold all the good they see. They give compliments when they are valid: "I had a really nice time. Let's do it again." If people share something about themselves that is cool, they validate that: "Wow, what an accomplishment. That must have felt good. I respect that kind of hard work." This is not a power move or loss. It is a sharing of yourself as a real person who is valuing the good in the other real person.

If you are not idealizing the other, then things are going to feel balanced. They can tell that you appreciate them, but that you don't need a hero to fix your life. They can tell that you have self-respect and that you don't act as if you are "above" liking them. In fact, healthy people like to know you enjoyed them. It gives them a reason to call you again or to want to go out again. Don't give so many compliments that they see you as a stalker, but don't unnaturally withhold what you feel.

One man told me that he really opened up to his wife when, after their second date, she called him right after he dropped her off from a lunch date. "It was not a big deal," he said. "She just said 'I just wanted to call and tell you that I really had a good time and enjoyed our talk. It was cool. Thanks for lunch. Have a good day.'

"She was just real and normal about it and seemed comfortable with herself. Also, I felt it gave me an open door. I could move ahead without all the gamey stuff. I did not have to wonder if she liked me or not. At the same time, I could tell she wasn't one of those stalker, dependent types. It was cool," he said.

Get a life. Stay balanced in your life, and just be yourself. Compliment what deserves complimenting. Confront what deserves confronting. Say yes to what deserves a yes and no to what deserves a no. If that is who you are, it will come through at a *chemical* level more than a *strategic* one. Be real, and if who you really are isn't a problem, then your strategy won't be one either.

22

Where Is the Testosterone?

I was having dinner with some married friends, and always being the researcher, I wanted to know how they got together. "How did you guys meet?" I asked.

They both started to laugh, so I knew I was in for a good story. "He comes off like the total stalker when you hear it," Anna replied.

I turned to Ben and asked, "What happened?"

"Well, I was at church one Sunday, and I saw her walk in with a couple who goes to my church. I thought, *Wow, she's cute. I have to go meet her*, since I had never seen her there before. After the service, I secretly moseyed on over to find her and not seem too conspicuous. But she was gone. Vanished. So, I started looking around for her, and I couldn't find her. At that point, I saw her getting into her car and starting to drive away.

"I couldn't let this happen, so I raced to my car, got in, and started chasing her down Pacific Coast Highway. It was so crowded

I weaved in and out of cars to catch her. Then I realized I didn't know what I would say to her once I caught up with her. And if I did catch her, she might think I was psycho and call the cops. So, I gave up the chase, thinking I had to find another way to meet her. I remembered that the couple she had come to church with had had a baby dedicated that day, so I figured they were my best shot. I would look for them and meet them to get to her.

"The next week I saw them, went up and introduced myself, and asked about their baby and made small talk, and a lot of other fluff just to get a chance to talk to them. I was on a mission; however, I didn't make my move then. I waited one more week before I struck up a friendly conversation with them again. Then I did it. I casually asked who that woman was with them a few weeks back. I said she seemed really nice, and I would love to meet her.

"At that point, the woman put me through the third degree! She totally interviewed me about my spiritual life, my intentions, the rest of my life, and the whole thing. She was on the lookout for her friend and did not want her with any slime balls. Evidently, I passed the interview, got a date, and here we are. But I tell you, it wasn't easy!"

On a Mission

I loved it. I hear this all the time from men who date well and finally find the woman of their dreams. They are initiators, and when she comes along, they are "on a mission." They are aggressive in going after what they want—not in some sort of Tarzan or obnoxious way, but *active* instead of *passive*. The key descriptor is *active initiators* instead of passive "hopers," hoping a woman will somehow fall into their life.

This is what I hear from women as well. They want men to initiate—before marriage and after. They are attracted to that quality in the beginning and for the long haul. Nothing is more like a cold shower to a woman than a man they have to lead around or push into decisions or activity, even when they act as if they would like to control him.

I asked one woman when she knew she first liked her husband. She said, "Funny thing. At first he seemed a little overly 'nice.' I thought that was fine, but I was not that attracted to him. Then, we went out to dinner on our first date, and this is going to sound strange, I know. But halfway through dinner, the waiter brought a dessert menu and placed it in the center of the table. We both grabbed it at the same time and pulled on it. It turned into a little of a tug of war, because we both wanted it. He took over, pulled it out of my hand, and smiled—winning the tug of war. Then he read it, asked me what I wanted, and ordered. This will sound strange, but *I knew I liked him when he did not let me win*."

This did not sound strange at all, because I have heard it a thousand times. Women want a man who is strong and assertive, but who *uses that assertiveness in service of the relationship*. He doesn't dominate her for selfish reasons, but he "wins," as she put it. Is this how to win a woman—grab things out of her hands and always come out on top? No, certainly not. But this was a *symbol* to her that he was strong enough *to not be controlled by her*. That is what she liked.

Call it whatever you want, but it is real. For the most part, men are designed to initiate, pursue, assert, protect, conquer, or whatever you want to call those traits that we refer to as masculine. I understand that women do all of these things too and that men should also be integrated with their "responding," more feminine parts. Men are to respond to a woman's initiating without feeling diminished. In fact, it is only with a strong man that a woman feels free to be her initiating, assertive self; however, she can't be assertive if he is not strong enough to not be controlled. If he is not, she can never fully be a woman, which includes being a responder. Although both sexes have initiating and responding parts, women are less attracted to men who don't initiate.

When asked about their relationships, women talk a lot about desiring to respond, desiring to be pursued, wanted, initiated with, and so forth. It helps them feel soft, sexual, *and* aggressive. A man's strength allows her to be all she is created to be. So, guys, wake up. God gave you testosterone, so use it. Step out, initiate, pursue, and stop being so passive.

When I was telling a psychologist friend of mine about this book, the first thing he said was, "Would you tell the men to stop whining about women only wanting someone with a paycheck, or status, or other such nonsense?" I could not agree more. Passive men say such things when they are not strong enough to attract a woman through the strength of their *personhood*. They feel as though they have to depend on symbolic expressions of power, like wealth or position, instead of interpersonal expressions of power.

A man's work and career has meaning to most women, but it is not about piles of money or titles or degrees. It is about the passionate, aggressive pursuit of what they care about. It is about the power of their character. If that passion ends up building a large company or a fulfilling career as a schoolteacher, the position doesn't matter. What she wants to see is that he is someone who pursues what he wants. That is attractive.

I was talking to Jade, a woman in her early thirties who is frustrated with a guy in her life. She has known him for three years, and they are very good friends. She takes him to events when she doesn't have a date, and vice versa. They are each other's "fill-in" date. They hang out, and their friends always wonder why they don't go for it. I asked the same thing.

"It's weird," she said. "I would like to find out if we could have something more or not. And I know he would too, 'cause he always makes comments when I talk about people I date, like 'If I were dating you, I would do this or that,' compared to what my boyfriends do. I know he has interest. But he is so not about showing it that I have never really seen him as someone who 'does it for me.' I like him, but there is no 'pizzazz.' He asks me to things without taking any risk. He'll casually ask, 'If you aren't doing anything, why don't we go to a movie?' It isn't like a date. It is like one of my girlfriends and I going somewhere when we don't have a date."

"Okay," I said, "let me ask you something. If he were to come right out, knock on your door, and say, 'Enough of this. We are going to date. Full out dating. We have been playing at this for too long. What are you doing Friday night? This is a real date I am talking about, not just hanging out because we have nothing else going on. I am asking you out. Boy meets girl!' What would you feel then?"

Jade blushed and said, "Oh, my gosh. I think I am getting a little excited just thinking about it." It was kind of funny to watch her blush.

"So," I replied, "Here is what you do. Call him and say, 'Justin, I want to know something. The other night you got a little friendly with me, kinda flirty. What do you want? Do you want to be friends, or do you want to date? Make up your mind. You are walking a fence, and I want to know what you want. Straight out. Either be my friend, or ask me out. I want to know, and I don't want an answer now. Think about it and call me like a grown up and ask me out, or tell me we are going to be just friends. And if we are friends, great. But stop acting as though there might be more if there is not.'"

"Awesome!" she said. "I am going to do it. I am sick of this, and it is time for him to stand up and be a real man."

I could not have said it better than that. Why was she not feeling any "pizzazz," as she put it? Was he attractive? Yes. Accomplished? Yes. Nice? Yes. All her friends and family loved him. Her parents lobbied for him. But he did not display his testosterone, his initiative, his aggression. So she had nothing to feel pizzazz in response to. She was not asking to be dominated. She was asking to be:

- wanted without fear
- desired without hesitancy
- pursued without waiting
- taken care of with forethought and planning
- initiated toward so she could respond.

When Jade finally did call Justin to assert that he either be her friend or ask her out, she found him in Vegas shacking up with a mutual friend of theirs. This is a good window into why one should be wary of passive men: They are often duplicitous. Jade said later that this was a great confirmation of why she had not been free to truly want Justin.

Go for It

What I am saying, guys, is that you have to know what you want and go for it. There is power in intention, power in desire, power in initiative. You do not have to be Tarzan or the Terminator. Here is the formula: *You have to have desire that you pursue.* This is the essence of the testosterone God created in you and to which she is wired to respond.

This is often the answer to the single man's dilemma of wanting the "idealized" woman and not being able to have her, or wanting one that is emotionally detached and unable to be captured. When he wants a woman he can't seem to land, he usually, at the same time, has a lot of women who want him but whom he is not interested in. I hear this all the time. "The ones I want don't want me, and the ones I don't, do."

The reason often is that when he sees someone he wants, he shuts down his aggression and starts trying to please her instead of taking the menu out of her hand or saying what he wants and doesn't want. So she is not interested, and he pines away. All the while, with the ones he does not want, he is strong and assertive because he is not afraid. So he drives them crazy.

The single woman also faces this dilemma. There's a nice guy she loves like a brother, but she wishes she felt more for him. He is so cute, so nice, and would "make someone a wonderful catch." She asks herself, "Why am I not interested in him? He is so good. I always want the 'bad' ones." If the nice one would take charge, she might find her problem solved.

So, here is my advice. Guys, go for it. Don't take a little obstacle or lack of interest as the end of the line. Don't feel the need for her to pave the way to "know that it is safe." Step out and make something happen. When you run into a little resistance, push through it. Don't back off until the door is really closed. (Sometimes that is only after she has a ring on her finger!)

And, gals, if a guy is not pursuing you and you have really given him ample opportunity and even talked it through, move on. Something is wrong. He is either not attracted to you, or he is conflicted and you do not want to be in the driver's seat long-term. Let him get his stuff worked out, and he may come around, but let that be on his initiative. Do not try to jump-start a passive guy forever. They are very frustrating.

Sometimes really good guys need a little push or a little hint. To get them over the hump, they sometimes need to know you are interested and open. They are more on the shy side, and that is okay. Some guys need to feel safe to move forward, and then they do. The question is whether, given that safety, they finally get moving or not. If they do, great, nothing wrong with needing a little encouragement from a good woman. But, after giving a guy a thousand opportunities to take the hill, you might want to consider that you are with a passive guy who is only going to continue to frustrate you until he deals with his passivity. Go drop the hankie in front of a man who will pick it up.

So, in sum, guys, get moving. You are responsible for making something happen, and you can't let your fears stop you. She won't want someone who would allow that to happen anyway. Realize that you are going to face rejection, scrutiny, comparisons, competition, and all of that. In fact, your job in dating is to get as many rejections as possible! Ask a lot of women out and reach for the stars. I am serious. The more rejections you get, provided you are getting some acceptances as well, the more you are really working it. To get the numbers up, you have to be turned down too.

If no one ever says yes, ask your team what is wrong. Get feedback, and read chapter 27, "Look in the Mirror." You may be getting turned down for a reason. But successful daters get turned down a lot. Get used to that. Do not put your worth on the line when you ask out a woman. She may reject you for a thousand reasons that have nothing to do with you. So what? You have to get in that mindset so you can go for it.

Do not give a woman that much power in your life. Whether or not any one woman thinks you are cool means nothing in the larger scheme of things, and if your masculinity, or worth, or power, or lovability is on the line when you ask someone out, you have to change that. Get loved and validated from God and from the people who know you and love you, not from some woman you are asking out. Get strong enough so when you are rejected or hit an obstacle, you are able to shrug it off and keep moving forward. That is the kind of man "the woman of your dreams" is looking for anyway, and that is the way you are going to find her.

Get your team together, work out your fears, and step up to the plate. She is waiting for you!

Keep Your Boundaries and Don't Settle

I don't know what to do with my boyfriend," said Stephanie, who was calling into our radio show. "We are having problems."

"What kind of problems," I asked.

"Well, I love Joe a lot, but he is really not very into the spiritual life, which is very important to me. Sometimes he pushes me for sex, and my values are very important to me, so we get into a fight over being physical. And it doesn't seem as though I am a very high priority to him. I mean, we spend time together, but his hobbies and the things he likes seem to always get first place and I come in second."

"How long have you been with him?"

"Almost a year."

"So, what's the problem?" It seemed obvious to me that this guy was not ready for a commitment and that he had some character issues to boot. *So why wasn't she dealing with them?* I wondered. *Why did she even stay with him?*

"I love him, and I want us to get married, but these things are bothering me. I don't know what to do . . ." she said, her voice trailing off into disappointment. "Sometimes it seems as though I should end it."

"So, why don't you?"

"I told you. I love him."

"So?"

"So what? I don't think you should just throw away love. It's too precious when you find it."

"'Throw away love' is a pretty tough phrase," I said. "I don't think that's how I'd put it. But let me tell you what I'm hearing. I hear something from you that is very, very common. You have gotten the cart before the horse."

"How?"

"You are evaluating this relationship and whether or not you are going to commit to him by the wrong thing. You are evaluating it by your attachment to him *instead of* by what you value. Let me ask you something. What do you want in a husband?"

"I want someone who is committed to me, is spiritually compatible, lives out our values, stuff like that."

"Those are good things to want in someone you commit to. Now, if you had never met your boyfriend, and if I said to you, 'Stephanie, I have a guy for you to fall in love with and marry. I want to fix you up. He is available, and you will probably find him attractive. But he won't pay attention to you, he will pursue his interests over the relationship, he is not into keeping his spiritual values, he is spiritually passive, he will leave you alone a lot while he does his own thing and get bugged at you when you try to talk about it, and he will pressure you to have sex, even though he espouses the same morals you do and says he is committed to waiting until marriage. But I think you will love him.' What would you say? Do you want him?"

"No! I would ask you to find me someone else."

"Exactly, because your values and your senses would be *leading* your selection process instead of your attachment to him. But now, because you 'love him,' your attachment to him is getting in the way of seeing what you want and what is vitally important. You cannot lead with whether or not you are attached to someone. You have to be guided by your spiritual values and the things that make love last. I am not suggesting you 'throw love away.' I am suggesting that you *protect* love and require the character that makes it work. That is what values do—they protect and preserve love and all the good things in life."

"So what do I do?"

"You lead with your values and what you want. You say, 'Joe, I am looking for a certain kind of relationship with a certain kind of person. The person I will ultimately commit to is honest, loving, responsible, spiritually committed, able to value the relationship and me as well as his own interests, and respectful of my boundaries, and he lives out our spiritual values. That is who I want to be with. Right now, *that is not you.* You do not do these things, and we have talked about how you don't many times. You know what they are. So, until you are that person or seriously are becoming that person, I cannot be with you. I will wait for that person. I hope you do become that person. I want that person to be you. But right now you are not. Let me know if you become him. Until then, I have to move on.'

"That is what you do. If he gets it and goes to counseling, joins an accountability group, or does something to show you he is serious, then there is a chance. But even then, you have to watch to see how real his change is and if it lasts without your pushing it or being the impetus that keeps it going. But, remember, you are looking for a set of inner values. If a person does not meet those, *you do not get involved, and you certainly do not commit. Period.*"

"I get it. Lead with my values, not how I feel about him," she said, "even when how I feel about him is very strong."

"You got it," I said. "How strongly you *feel* is *not* the test."

Lead with Values

I see this problem over and over again in dating. It causes some people to abandon dating altogether. They get attached too soon, without good boundaries, and then this attachment clouds their judgment. Remember, the person you get involved with emotionally or make a commitment to, *must pass the values test.* He has to be able to fit through that gate. If he can't, then you must let go and move on, at least until he has faced his issues, and only then if he proves himself over time. Until then, guard your heart. Look for someone worth giving it to.

If you have reached the point where your attachment is confusing your values, look to your team. Submit to them and give them permission to tie you to a tree! They are there to save your life. Allow them to.

Remember that your values are there to protect you and to preserve your life. As Solomon said in Proverbs:

> *For wisdom will enter your heart,*
> *and knowledge will be pleasant to your soul.*
> *Discretion will protect you,*
> *and understanding will guard you.*
> *Wisdom will save you from the ways of wicked men,*
> *from men whose words are perverse,*
> *who leave the straight paths*
> *to walk in dark ways,*
> *who delight in doing wrong*
> *and rejoice in the perverseness of evil,*
> *whose paths are crooked*
> *and who are devious in their ways.*
> (Prov. 2:10–15)

Your values are the architecture of your dating life. Bind them around your neck and do what they tell you. They will lead you to the right one.

Keep Your Boundaries, Command Respect

The best way to avoid Stephanie's situation is to "nip it in the bud." Keep your boundaries and enforce them as soon as bad behavior enters into a relationship. If someone pushes you past your values, or wants, or choices, stand up and say no. If she does not respect your no, then tell her to go away until she gets it. If she protests, say, "What is it about no that you do not understand?"

The same goes for other disrespectful behavior. If he treats you like a nonperson or does not respect your time by always being late without calling or by being deceitful, stand up and say you will not tolerate that. The best way to assure you will find someone good is to *require* someone to be good. The bad ones will move on to someone else, and you will be open to the good.

Do not allow bad behavior. Remember, you get what you tolerate. If you need support to do that, get it. But don't allow bad things to reside in your dating life. Keep your boundaries, and do not settle for less than good behavior.

Part 3

Get Your Dating Self in Shape

Monitor Your Internal World and Face Your Issues

- "I turn into somebody else," Joel said. "It's weird. If I'm attracted to a woman, I retreat into my shell. I lose my way."
- "I don't get it," Missy said. "When I am at work, I talk to guys all the time. I'm funny, interactive, and pretty cool to be around, if I say so myself. But, get me around a cute guy and something happens inside. If I'm at a party, I go to the other side of the room."
- "I started out normal," Tonya said. "Then, as I talked to him, I noticed that the more I liked him, the more I thought about how big my rear end is right now. And I don't really think it is that big, but it started to feel like it. All I could do was obsess about what he must be thinking."

- "My friend wanted to set me up with someone," Alex told me. "But I started to think, *What if she's a geek? It will feel like one more failure.*"
- "I wanted to go up and talk to him, but I just felt that was being too aggressive," Paige told me when I asked her what she did at the party.
- "I looked at him and just figured he wasn't my type," Rebecca said. "He seemed like the kind that is really nice and all that, but not very much pizzazz."
- "I thought she was just so 'clean,'" Brian said. "I figured that if she really knew some of the stuff about me and my past, I wouldn't have a chance. Even though I am so much different now, someone like her wants 'the perfect guy.'"

Sound familiar? Maybe it's not these particular things that make up the noise in your head about dating. But if you are stuck, chances are that something unhelpful is going through your head. Remember our guiding principle about changing your dating life: The inside produces the outside. If you are stuck in your dating life, some attitudes, fears, conflicts, and thinking inside of you may need a redo. When you listen to what is going on inside your head, you will have clues to what is keeping you stuck.

The following topics from the previous chapters are in no way exhaustive of the things that keep people stuck, but if you just go through some of the things we have already talked about (listed below) and ask yourself what you say to yourself about these issues, you may find some interesting stuff lurking in your head. Here are a few examples of unhelpful things some people say to themselves related to the issues:

- Blaming God or circumstances: "Why doesn't God bring someone to me?"
- Getting angry or discouraged when encouraged to take responsibility: "So you're saying it's all my fault. Great, one more way I'm a loser."

- Dating is a reflection of things going on inside of you: "How can I help it if no one is asking me out? I am not doing anything. I am open to people, but no one is calling." Or, "Of course. All of my failures are my fault. I can never do anything right."
- Lack of prospects is not the problem: "I have met everyone at my church and in my circle of friends. This place really has no available singles."
- Be accountable to others about dating: "What good is an accountability group going to do me if there is no one I am dating anyway? What would I share with people?"
- Keep a log of your dating action: "That seems ridiculous. That won't help. Too much work."
- Meet five a week: "I would not like people I met randomly." "That's impossible." "I am too shy to meet new people." "They won't like me."
- Don't limit yourself to a type: "I know what I like. I don't want to go out with someone I am not into."
- Go out with almost anyone once or twice: "Why waste my time?"
- Get rid of expectations: "I have to have someone who has an advanced degree." "If I did not marry a blonde, I would feel like I am settling for less." "I want tall."
- Be yourself: "I get so nervous. Why don't I just speak up?" "I am so different with my friends than when I am talking to someone I might go out with."
- Join an online dating service: "No way would I do that. That is so slimy."
- Don't play games: "You have to play the game. You can't just lay all your cards on the table."
- Change your traffic patterns: "That will never work. I won't meet anyone at a stupid softball game."
- Take a look at your internal world: "I don't want to look inward. I just want to fall in love."

To look at yourself in these areas could keep you busy for a while. You may have a lot of work to do. But what I find is that when people begin to get unstuck, they do that work. They find out what is really going on when they approach dating, when they are on a date, or when they withdraw from dating. They talk about those things with their team, and they take steps to change. In short, they monitor their internal world and change it.

God promises to give you wisdom when you persevere through a problem or a trial (James 1:2–5). Certainly your dating life qualifies as a place where you have trials and need some wisdom to know what to do and how to change. Ask God to help you, and get busy.

Here are some common areas that often need some attention:

- Fears of intimacy that lead to being attracted only to fantasy, idealized love objects: "When I get close, I get disinterested, or afraid."
- Fears of being controlled that cause people to flee commitment and real relationships: "I begin to feel smothered or closed in." "When they like me, I lose interest."
- Fears of one's imperfections and flaws, and a lack of self-acceptance: "I feel as if I am not attractive enough to get someone to like me." "If she knows that about me, she would never like me." "He is not handsome or spiritual or accomplished enough."
- Fears of one's sexuality that leads to repression and a lack of being attracted to, or being attractive to, the opposite sex: "I shouldn't feel that way." "I don't feel sexual feelings too much."
- Body image problems that cause interpersonal fears: "I am too fat." "I am too skinny." "I am too short, tall, ugly, or whatever."
- Abuse issues that have never been faced: "I am afraid of people."
- Lack of assertiveness that leads to fears of people: "I get scared to say no."

- Rampant impulsive sexuality that makes love, intimacy, and real relationship impossible: "I just want sex."
- Having impossibly high standards that are really designed to keep you protected from available people: "She's not smart enough." "He's not tall enough."
- Having rigid religious rules and issues that have nothing to do with spiritual maturity or the Bible: "He doesn't fit my idea of a godly man." "It's not spiritually mature to flirt or be on the hunt."

I just got an email from a woman I coached who at one time had zero dates. It had been that way for two years. She worked the program, was dating in a few months, and got married after a couple of years. Now she takes her friends through the steps you are reading about in this book. She called me very excited because one of the women she was coaching married this past weekend. It was a joyous occasion for all of them. When I got the email, I was writing this chapter, and I could not help but smile when I remembered this step in her path.

When I had her monitor her internal world, the issues that came up really surprised her. For example, being a successful businesswoman, she had no idea that she felt vulnerable around men and afraid of rejection. But when I had her meet five men a week, she would tell me, "It was so *weird*. When I began talking to a man I had never met, all I could think about was my weight, my skin, how I looked, and a bunch of other stuff about appearance. In work, I never do that. But I noticed that in this arena, I was really self-conscious, and I would not be myself. It is no wonder why they are not asking me out. There is no one there!"

So she joined a group of friends and went through the *Changes That Heal* book and workbook, which looks at underlying issues that cause these fears. She saw how family patterns of rejection and criticism had affected her and how she had never really dealt with them. The hurt she was walking around with had to be healed. This hurt not only caused her to expect more of the same kind of rejection, but also caused her to give up on her body as well—she didn't keep in shape and gained weight. She did not really want to be vulnerable again.

However, as she looked at those patterns, cried out some hurt, allowed others in the group to be there for her, and love her for who she was, she reclaimed her body, her sexuality, and her confidence. She stopped seeing men through the lens of her past rejection. And they started to see her, for the first time in a long time. Dating began. She lost weight and became more of herself with men. It was fun to go through the program with her.

This is what I mean by finding out what is going on inside and working on it. It is an example of the proverb we read earlier: "Guard your heart with all diligence, for from it flow the issues of life" (Prov. 4:32 KJV). Her issues of no dates were connected to things in her heart that she had not dealt with until then.

But that is not all. The email was telling in another way. While she was thrilled about the woman she was coaching getting married, *she also noticed how people who are not dealing with their internal issues are contributing to their lack of dates.* She was so concerned about them that she wrote the following email to make sure I addressed the problem in this book!

> *After a bachelorette party, my married friend Robin and I were talking to Leah (a cute red head who is a part of the dating group). All the other girls had left, but we were still sitting in the lounge. We were encouraging Leah to meet guys. After about forty-five minutes of this, Leah finally said, "But, Steph, you are an extrovert, and it's easy for you to meet guys!"*
>
> *I said, "Leah, you did not know me before Henry! I would never have done that before. I learned how to be more inviting to guys. I was closed off, and like you, never would have initiated conversations with guys!"*
>
> *So, Henry, how can you address the "introverts"?* **Being an introvert is no excuse.** *She did well with me back when we were both going out, because I did help get her into conversa-*

tions. I made eye contact with guys so they would come over and talk to us. Even that very night during the party, I said, "Leah, there are guys wanting to come talk to us (party of ten girls), but I was the only one making eye contact because I am so used to it, and I had to keep looking back down because I am married."

But, finally, two guys came over twice trying to talk to us. But, all the available girls were so NOT open. The ones who were open were either dating someone steadily or engaged, and they didn't care to talk to the guys. The others, who claim to really want to meet someone, were just clueless and missed an opportunity. It was so characteristic of women NOT seeing what's going on around them!

This woman has been there. When she had looked at her internal world, she had found out why she was stuck. Now she is able to see it in her women friends and is coaching them! It is so clear to her why some of them are stuck, now that she can see. This illustrates the principle of Jesus' words, "First take the plank out of your own eye, and then you can see clearly to remove the speck from the other person's eye" (Matt. 7:5). We see others most clearly after we do the hard work of looking at ourselves first. To look inside and listen to what is in your head is the first step. Then, to deal with it is to have a new life.

I love it when this woman does not let her friends off the hook, as she did not let herself. She knows what it is like to be held back by her problems, but also to push through them, and she will not allow the ones she loves to stay stuck as she was. She won't allow the "others who claim to really want to meet someone" to remain "clueless" and miss an "opportunity." She wants them to stop being "women who are not seeing what's going on around them!" Good words.

So, here is my advice, as well as hers and that of others who have turned their dating lives around:

- Get active in the program and then watch what that brings up inside. Monitor it, observe it, and learn what is happening.

- Deal with what you find inside. Talk to a friend, counselor, or someone who can help you heal and change whatever is holding you back.

In the next chapter we will look at what issues may be holding you back and what to do about them.

Get Healthy

A group of friends and I were having dinner one night, and the conversation turned to dating and the single life. Abby knew I coached singles on dating, so she asked me a question many people have asked: "Why is it that I always attract the ones I'm not interested in, and the ones I want are not attracted to me?"

"How are you different when you are with the ones you like?" I asked.

"I have that job-interview kind of feeling," Abby replied. "Like I'm sitting there wondering if I will get the 'callback' for the second interview. I hate that 'callback' feeling. It makes me hate first dates so much, 'cause I am wondering about the second one."

"What if you went on the date for its own sake?"

"I would still be worried about dealing with the second-date problem."

"What do you mean?"

"Well, if he likes you and wants to ask you out again, how do you say no if you don't like him? Either way, the first date is awkward, whether you are worried you won't get a second date or worried you will."

A happily married thirty-five-year-old woman sitting at the table spoke up at this point. "If he asks you out again, it doesn't matter what he thinks. If you don't want to go, tell him you aren't interested! That's a no-brainer," she said. "Why are you more concerned with what he thinks than with what you want anyway?"

"Stop!" I said. "Please say that again." The non-professional had just said it better than the psychologist could have. She was happily married, but had loved dating when she was single. And she had just explained why: *She was not caught up in what the guys thought of her. She knew who she was and what she wanted and what she didn't want, and she was not shy about saying it.*

Then I said something to Abby that had never occurred to her. "That's the answer to the first question you asked about why the ones you want don't want you and why you don't want the ones who want you."

"How so?" she asked.

"You are conflicted about what *you* want and don't want. When you don't want a guy, it's hard for you to tell him—nicely, but clearly and directly. When you *are* attracted to someone, you mold and adapt instead of being clear inside yourself and confident about who you are and what you want. Your adapting blocks the man from seeing you for who you really are, so the guy has nothing to be attracted to. He moves on.

"At other times, when you don't care so much, you are more yourself, and those guys just *love* you. But even then, when they do, you can't tell them you are *not* interested. Your 'adaptive' stuff comes back in. When you get over worrying about other people's feelings to the exclusion of what you want, you will attract the right guys."

This was a little hard for her to understand at first. But the more we talked, the more she admitted she always took responsibility for her family's feelings, especially those of her father, not wanting to disappoint him. She had become the classic "people pleaser." And it came out the most whenever she was with a man whose approval she desired. It was just like when she desired her father's approval, she became her adaptive self with him instead of her real self. She did the same with other men, and it was ruining her dating life. It kept her from displaying the attractiveness of her God-given personality. To change her dating life, she would have to get healthy.

Attracting the Ones You Want

At any juncture in life we have many things to work out in our personal lives. We are always growing and changing. But dating is not that complicated. You don't have to be a picture of health to attract people and have successful relationships, but you do have to have some basic issues aligned in ways that do not get in the way. Let's take a look at what some of those are.

While this is not a book on how to get emotionally healthy, *you need a certain amount of health to do the two things the title of this book suggests*—get dates, and get dates worth keeping. You want to attract people of the opposite sex, and you want to attract the ones worth attracting. So, what are the important issues? And how do you resolve those?

I have written extensively about issues of personal growth. I can't repeat all that here, but I can touch on some recurring issues that lead to dating problems. Paying attention to these few areas can bear great fruit, while ignoring them can bring lots of heartache, from not finding dates to finding bad ones. Below are the important issues.

Develop Emotional Connectedness

To connect emotionally means to be present with your heart, mind, and soul in relationship to others. It means to be open and vulnerable in a way that your heart, mind, and soul are available *to be known and experienced by others*. It means being able to trust and need another person. It means being able to invest emotionally in someone.

If you are not able to do that or are limited in some significant way, one of two things will happen. First, you will not have enough emotional presence to draw someone in and to "hook" that person's interest or desire. Second, if you do attract someone, you are going to attract someone who is looking for, or only able to relate to, a detached or unavailable person.

If you have trouble connecting emotionally with people, get in a *nondating* environment of safe people and work through your fears of being known. Learn to need them. Be vulnerable to them. Share yourself with them. Get close. Trust. Talk about your fears of doing all of that and where those fears came from. Getting more emotionally available will help your dating life. I can't stress how important it is to do this in a nondating context.

You can do this with a small group, a therapist, a therapy group, or a growth group of friends. You can structure your time with workbooks or other study guides. There are a lot of ways, but get real and get healed of your disconnectedness in nonromantic settings first if you want to connect with someone romantically. Here are some skills to practice:

- Realize your need.
- Move toward others, reach out.
- Be vulnerable.
- Challenge distorted thinking.
- Say yes to life.
- Allow dependent feelings.
- Recognize defenses.
- Become comfortable with anger.
- Take risks.
- Pray.
- Express empathy to others.

As you become more of a connecting person with your support system, you will be more connectable in dating. Emotional availability in a good and healthy way will flow from you. In addition, *you won't be lonely. You will be grounded in these supportive and healing relationships.* Because of that, you won't make bad choices in dating just to end your loneliness.

Establish Good Boundaries

To have good boundaries means that you know where you end and another person begins. You know what you want and don't want. You know how to set limits and say "no." If someone is hurting you, you know how to say, "Stop that!" or "I don't like that." You know how to say, "I'm not comfortable with that, and I don't want to participate."

When you have good boundaries, you are honest, clear, direct, and able to confront when necessary. It means you are clear about not only the negative, but also the positive. It means being clear about who you are and being able to express directly what you want.

If you cannot do this, several bad things can happen in dating.

First, you will be passive and unattractive. People value people who respect themselves and do not easily give in to them. If you are too "easy," you will not be attractive, at least not for long.

Second, you will not be independent enough to attract a healthy person. As I said earlier, independence and separateness creates attraction. Boundaries create autonomy, which creates freedom, which is essential for attraction and love. This is why the ones who are "hard to get" are so attractive: Their independence and freedom are so alluring. Without good boundaries, you will not attract.

This is also why so many dating books tell you not to be so available for a date, to keep your distance, or to play hard to get. While I don't think these strategies are the answer (see chapter 21, "Don't Play Games"), people find them helpful because they make them appear separate. Boundaries do a better job of creating healthy space than games and manipulation.

Third, you might attract someone controlling or abusive. People who are controlling find those whom they can control. If they can't control a person, they move on. If you do not have good boundaries, you are a magnet for a controlling or self-centered person.

Finally, you will control others and not respect their independence. People without good boundaries are subtle controllers of others, often in dependent and smothering ways. If you do this to people you date, especially early on, you will chase them away. You will lose them very soon, and if not soon, then as soon as the relationship is serious. Ultimately people will not allow themselves to be controlled. So don't even start.

Thus, just as you did with emotional connectedness, find a good place in nonromantic relationships to learn and practice the following skills:

- Gain awareness of what you like and don't like, what you want and don't want.
- Define who you are and are not.
- Develop your "no" muscle.
- Stop blaming others.
- Stop playing the victim.
- Persevere and develop self-discipline.
- Become proactive, not reactive.
- Set limits.
- Choose and enforce your values.
- Accept others' choices and don't control them.
- Realize your separateness and independence from others.
- Be honest, clear, and direct.
- Challenge distorted thinking.
- Practice self-control with help from others.

Accept Reality

Let's face it. You would love to be ideal, perfect, and heavenly. You would like to have the looks and body of the latest movie star, the heart of Mother Teresa, the intellect of Stephen Hawking, or the wit of your favorite comedic figure. But the reality is that you are attractive in your own way, have a good but imperfect heart, are smart enough to do what you do, and find humor in your own way. And guess what? These things would be very, very, attractive—in fact *intoxicating*—to the right person. Just who you are—not perfect, but juicy and real.

But, if you don't feel you are attractive, you won't be. If you feel as though you aren't good enough and would only be good enough if you were your ideal, then the real you *won't* be attractive to that very same right person. He or she won't ever see you because the real you will be hidden by anxiety, performance issues, fears of rejection, narcissism, hiding, and defenses—all of the things we call insecurity. If you feel you are not good enough, you won't be. Not because you aren't, but because you don't feel as if you are, and you show it.

In addition, you will look for the "ideal" or the perfect person to make up for what you feel is lacking in yourself. And this is never attainable. As soon as you've found the perfect person, he or she will disappoint and not be good enough. So you will always be alone and looking, too picky, or you will be attracted to those who try to appear ideal and perfect but have made themselves unattainable. You will chase them and never catch them, as it is their strategy, like yours, to never be caught.

Instead of that scenario, you could join reality and learn to accept your good parts, your bad parts, your imperfections, and the real you. You can be known in your hurts and your failures. Then you would be loved as you are, and you would have nothing left to prove. You could "take off the fig leaf" and stop hiding. Then there would be a *lot to be attracted to.* Those parts would be real, touchable, able to be experienced, sexy, juicy, life-giving, interesting, and all of the other real things God has placed inside every human soul, *if they can be seen by others.*

But to do that, you must come out of self-judgment and be known and loved by others as you really are, first in a *nondating* context. Get into a relational setting such as I mentioned above and practice these skills:

- Confess your faults and imperfections.
- Talk about the things you feel the worst about.
- Pray together about them.
- Practice loving what is less than ideal and perfect in others.
- Do not discard others when they are less than perfect.
- Accept your failures and others when they fail.
- Process negative feelings, like sadness, anger, hurt, and fear.
- Don't expect perfection in yourself, others, or the world around you.
- Forgive everyone.

- Rework your ideal and have it be a real person and not a fantasy.
- Rework distortions in the way you evaluate yourself.
- Monitor the way you talk to yourself about your imperfections.

Grow Up and Become Equal with Others

If you want a disaster recipe for dating, try dating adults while feeling like a child inside. You will go into every relationship feeling "one down," inferior, not good enough, looking for approval, powerless, confused, judged, and sexually hung up.

If you want to find a good relationship, grow up and take hold of adulthood. Stop putting yourself in either the child or the parent position with others. Value your thoughts and opinions and speak your mind, but also respect the opinions of others. Give up wanting other people's approval, and stop giving them the power to make you feel good about yourself. Give up judging others or allowing their judgments to affect you.

View your sexuality as an adult. Stop seeing it as something to feel ashamed of, and stop idealizing it as if it were what life is made for and acting out as if you can't delay gratification any longer than a two-year-old. If you repress sexuality as a child does, you won't attract anyone and you'll come across like a cold fish. If you express sexuality all the time, you will look like a trampy teenager without parents at home, and no one will take you seriously, other than for a one-night fantasy. This is not what you are after.

Respect authority and stop rebelling, but at the same time don't idealize authority and turn authority figures into parents. Disagree and have your own opinions about things. As a result, you will become your own authority in your own areas of expertise, developing your talents, hobbies, interests, and career. This makes you an interesting person with whom someone would like to go out and enjoy getting to know—a mutual, equal, competent adult.

See yourself as an equal in every relationship. Even when you play a nonequal role with someone, you still see yourself as an equal human being. For example, you respect your boss's authority, but you are self-assured, and your thoughts and opinions are just as valid as those of your boss. You have mutual respect.

What often happens in dating is that people place themselves in an inferior position. They cow-tow to dates, looking up to them, giving them sick power as they look for their approval. This not only sets up horrible dynamics but also kills attraction. Self-confidence is a turn-on, in a good way. Overly passive submission (which is quite different than biblical submission or meekness) causes both men and women to lose their attractiveness to those who would otherwise find them very interesting.

Remaining a child is destructive to dating and devastating to marriage. (I go into this in much more detail in my book *Changes That Heal*.) It is imperative that you work out these issues for dating to go well, including not only getting "chosen," but choosing well. Here are some things to work on to become an equal person in a relationship:

- Reevaluate your beliefs and decide for yourself.
- Disagree with authority figures.
- See parents and authority figures realistically.
- Make your own decisions.
- Practice disagreeing.
- Deal with your sexuality.
- Give yourself permission to be equal with your parents.
- Recognize and pursue your talents.
- Practice.
- Recognize the privileges of adulthood.
- Discipline yourself.
- Say no to bad stuff.
- Submit to others out of freedom.
- Do good works.
- Love people who are different.

As you do these things, you will no longer be "one down" to some fantasized parent figure. You won't treat your dates like a wished-for mommy or daddy. They will appreciate that—and you. So what do you look like when you are healthy?

- You can make an emotional connection.
- You have self-respect and clear boundaries. People know where you stand and what you want.
- You are real and feel okay about yourself. You don't have to be perfect or find a perfect person.
- You are competent and have opinions and talents of your own, and you treat others as equals.
- You are comfortable with your sexuality, but not acting it out like a teenager.

Put all that in front of another healthy person, and you are likely to find yourself going out. Omit those things, and you are likely to not be noticed, or if you are, you might not like what you get.

26

Don't Be Dr. Jekyll and Mr. Hyde

Rich was frustrated with his dating life, complaining to me about there not "being any good women out there," then went on to tell me about his latest relationship that had gone sour. I could have stopped him halfway through and told the rest of the story myself. Why? I had heard it all before. Where? From him. Several times. Here is the story as he told it.

"I don't get it," he said. "I met her, and she was really nice and attractive. She was so kind and easy to be around. She really appreciated me and our time together, and we had a wonderful time. I took great care of her. I bought her things, took her places, and treated her as well as anyone could want.

"Then, later, I find out that she hasn't been up front with me about some stuff. She has all this stuff going on with an old boyfriend. Not that she likes him, but he is kind of a business partner and she did not tell me that. She still talks to him more than is healthy.

"Also, she is not as into God as she led me to believe. Much of her spiritual life comes from me. She acted as if she was into following God, but I see she is into other things more as time goes on. Plus, I don't like the way she lets her kid get away with things. She won't discipline him. And she won't tell me the straight truth about other things either. I find out a lot later. She's just not a straight-up character," he bemoaned.

"The longer we went out, the more she changed. She started wanting to have things her way. Women are all like that. They turn selfish on you after a while. I don't get it."

I sighed. I had hoped Rich could make dating work for him and could have what he wanted—a good marriage. He is a good guy, has good values, and has a lot to give. But it was going to take a bulldozer to get him to realize the real problem, and it was going to be an uphill ride.

What was wrong with Rich? *He was not a balanced person, so he attracted imbalanced people.*

In a sense, he caused the problems he bemoaned. He was not Dr. Jekyll and Mr. Hyde, but he was half of a person. Rich was Tarzan, and he wanted his women to be Jane.

Rich loved taking care of women. He would swoop in like Tarzan swinging on a vine, rescue them from whatever situation they found themselves in, and be their hero. He would make all the decisions, and he would be strong and dependable. "What a catch!" they would feel.

But they did not see his inability to allow them to disagree or have an opinion. He could not yield to another person. He could not show weakness or vulnerability. He would make up for that inflexibility by being a very attractive "strong man" to women who would want to be swept off their feet more than they wanted a real person.

So, they would be a perfect match—until he would see the other side of a passive, compliant woman. She would be sneaky and not tell him exactly what was going on. Then, lo and behold, one day she would really "mess up" and have a wish contrary to something he wanted or valued. Then, from his perspective, she had "changed" and had become "selfish." "She used to be nice, and now look!"

But in reality, this is not what had happened. She had not changed. When they first met, she showed only half of who she was, hiding the other half, which would come out in sneaky, indirect ways. After a while, it came out directly, such as when she disagreed with him. Then he would cry, "Foul."

So they both got what they asked for. In her compliance, she attracted a controller. In his control he attracted an adaptive person who had a secret side and was indirect. They were co-conspirators, and it always blew up.

Is there any hope for Rich and his dates? Certainly. But some things would have to change. He would have to give up the need to be totally in control and learn to share power, and he would also need to show weakness and vulnerability instead of masking it with macho control. She would have to not be so adaptive from the beginning and show a sense of self-control instead of giving it all up to Tarzan in exchange for being rescued. If they did that, they would both attract more balanced people. If they did it at the same time, they might even like each other.

So, the key is to resolve your splits. A "split" is common. It just means that you have opposing parts of yourself that have not come together. As a result, you live out of only a part of yourself and not all of who you are at any given moment. Usually a "split" shows itself as being on one end of a continuum, such as active vs. passive, feeling vs. thinking, insecure vs. confident, or strong vs. weak. If you find yourself on one side of a continuum, your dating life will suffer, and you will attract the wrong type.

Another way this problem manifests itself is when people display both sides of themselves but in different areas *with different people.* For example, they are spiritual with a certain set of people and "worldly" with another. If you do this, you are two people, and whom will you date? Anyone you date is only going to get half of you. If you choose from your "sinner" identity, then what about your "saintly" parts? Are you really going to like that "bad boy" forever?

Further, if the person you like is a whole person, it won't work. He will not like you, since you are only a "half." If you came forth with both sides of yourself and got real, you would have a greater chance of attracting another whole person. Solomon said it this way:

> Do not be overrighteous,
>   neither be overwise—
>   why destroy yourself?
> Do not be overwicked,
>   and do not be a fool—
>   why die before your time?
> It is good to grasp the one
>   and not let go of the other.
>   (Eccl. 7:16–18)

The real lesson here regarding good parts and bad parts is in the last line, and it is also true of all splits: "It is good to grasp the one and not let go of the other." Rich and his girlfriend had not done that in their own personalities. She had gone totally submissive to the Tarzan type, not standing up for her own wishes and thoughts, and he had gone totally into being in control. So, it would not work. That is why they could walk away wondering, "Why am I always attracted to the wrong type?" Think of the extremes you need to avoid and bring both parts of yourself to a relationship:

- Your desires to be spiritual and holy, and your failures and imperfections
- Your strengths and your weaknesses
- Your successes and your failures
- Your happiness and your struggles
- Your talents and your inabilities
- Your sexuality and your values
- Your ability to dress up and look good, and your casual side
- Your connected parts and your loneliness
- Your "holiness" and your sin
- Your independence and your dependent feelings

- Your victories and your defeats
- Your confidence and your insecurity

To the extent you are split, you will find the wrong type. Or, you won't be able to land the one you are looking for.

Why You Attract the Wrong Type

Besides splits, people are attracted to the wrong types for other reasons. Here are some for you to think about. (For a more detailed treatment of these, take a look at the book *Safe People*, which I cowrote with Dr. John Townsend.) Being drawn to the wrong type, or attracting the wrong type, is no accident. Take ownership of your patterns and find out why. If you do that, you can work through the reasons and change your pattern.

- *Inability to judge character.* Use your head and your values, in addition to your heart, to choose a person to date based on character. Get your head and heart on the same page. Often your heart can fool you when your attraction to a person comes out of only your feelings. When you are in that mode, you disregard the data that your head is feeding you about the person's character. You can see enough to be cautious or even run the other way, but because of how you "feel," you ignore what your head is telling you.
- *Isolation and fear of abandonment.* Choosing dates from a lonely place inside draws you to people who can't connect, or it makes you so desperate that you connect with anyone who will have you, no matter what they are like, in order to not be alone. A "bad" relationship feels better than none at all. Get connected to some good people outside of dating, and you won't feel so alone and desperate.
- *Defensive hope.* You may have been hurt or let down by a certain type of person in your life (often a parent), and you are still hoping to get that person to change, and to love you. So you are drawn to people like him or her with the hope that you can finally heal that problem relationship. The sad thing

is that these people are also drawn to you, because your dynamics work with their dysfunction, similar to the parent or other significant person who taught you how to play the game. Resolve your old business through forgiveness and grief, letting go of what you can never have from that kind of person who hurt you. Get what you need from good people in nondating, healing relationships, and then you won't have to defend against the loss anymore. It is finished.

- *Unfaced badness.* If you have not faced your "bad parts" and feel as if you have to be "all good," you might be drawn to the "bad boy" or "bad girl" type to find completion and to allow someone else to express those bad parts for you. Not facing your badness keeps you from owning it, with the resulting guilt and fear. Accept your bad parts, get forgiven, and be real. Then you won't need a bad boy or bad girl.

- *Merger wishes.* You "merge" with a someone to find the parts you do not have. For example, if you are passive, you might be drawn to someone really aggressive and "strong." This gives you a sense of having what you don't have. If you are adaptive, you might be drawn to a controller, like the classic codependent. If you are cut off and have to be "strong," you might attract needy people with "problems." Merging is an attempt to get missing parts. Develop the side of you that is missing or not being owned. Then you won't have to shop for yourself.

- *Fear of confrontation.* If you can't confront, the person who doesn't like to be confronted will find you. It is like magic. But people who don't like to be confronted are not only very selfish; they are also in denial, and they are unable to resolve conflict. Not fun people to date. Learn to be assertive and confront appropriately, and they will flee you and the good ones will find you.

- *Romanticizing.* You turn everything into a romantic fantasy and block out reality, so you don't see the reality of the person you are drooling over. While you are noticing the moonlight, use that light to see the whole person and sit with the reality of who they truly are. Let that settle in, and you might or might not want to be there for long. Vampires only come out at night.

- *Need to rescue.* As a rescuer, you have to find a person with problems. You might as well drive an ambulance and get dates that way. Learn to give to people in service settings instead of in dating. Stop rescuing people from problems they should be taking responsibility for themselves. Hold people responsible for their own lives, and you won't need to marry a problem. Get help for your codependent patterns.

- *Familiarity.* You have learned dysfunctional dynamics in a dysfunctional relational setting, such as the family you grew up in, and you have gotten programmed to operate that way. So, a normal person does not fit into your program. It's time to reprogram yourself. Learn healthy relationship patterns in healing settings, such as a small group.

- *Victim role.* You have learned to take whatever comes and you think you have no choices in life and relationships. Get back in touch with the reality that you are not a child any more and that you have lots of options open to you other than mistreatment or someone who is not good for you.

- *Guilt.* Unresolved guilt can draw you to someone who dishes out guilt and makes you feel bad about yourself. Go somewhere and work out your guilt so you won't need a fresh supply every day to remind you how you fall short.

- *Perfectionism.* If you demand perfection in yourself, you might be drawn to someone who is similarly demanding and much more verbal about it. So you will never be good enough. Learn to accept yourself, and if someone can't accept you, empathize with how frustrating that must be to them to be in a relationship with an imperfect person!

- *Denial of pain and perceptions.* You might have learned to not notice what you notice. You numb yourself to that little voice inside that sees that something is not right. Or you ignore that feeling that says "This does not feel good," and you keep going. Reclaim your senses and feelings: "Solid food is for the mature, who because of practice have their senses trained to discern good and evil" (Heb. 5:14, NASB). Retrain your senses.

- *Unintegrated sexuality.* Your sexuality has not been connected to love, relationship, and your values, so it has a life of its own. This can result in being attracted to a sex addict in disguise, or to having highly charged sexual connections or attractions to people who do not have the ability to connect. Integrate your sexuality to the rest of you so you attract a whole person.

Even though it seems as though there are a lot of reasons why people pick the wrong person, there is really only one: *not becoming a whole person.* No matter what you have negated in yourself, you can integrate those parts by talking about them with a good therapist, group, friends, God, and others.

When you work through your "stuff," you won't need a bad character in your movie any more, because the script will be a different one. If your life is no longer a tragedy, you won't need a villain. If it is no longer a comedy, you won't need a flake. If it is no longer a disaster story, you won't need someone who produces crises. If it is no longer a seedy sex thriller, you won't need an addict.

When your life becomes one of healthy friends who have healed the parts of you that needed healing and growth, your outside world will reflect that as well. A healthy movie always requires good characters! So, as you get healthy, people will audition for those parts in your life that your health requires.

27

Look in the Mirror

At a seminar I was leading, a woman raised her hand and said that she thought the problem in dating was that men were only interested in appearance, and she found that to be really shallow. The last man she was interested in, she said, was not interested in her, and she surmised that it was because of her weight.

It did not take long for the audience and me to hear that she was angry. "Men are so conditional in the way they love. I want to find unconditional love and be accepted for who I am as a person. That is like God's love," she said. "I think you should focus on teaching men how to love unconditionally."

"What is it you want?" I asked.

"What do you mean?"

"I mean, what are you looking for? Do you want to get married? Is that what you want?"

"Yes, I do. I want a man to love and to share my life with. But he needs to love me as I am, weight and all."

"Okay, I will find you a husband by next Monday. Can you be here? Bring a preacher, and I will have a husband for you by next week."

"What!!?? What do you mean?"

"Well, you said you wanted to get married, and I'm sure I can find someone for you to marry by next week. So be here, and we can do the ceremony."

"Well, what . . . I mean, who would it be?"

"I don't know; I will find someone. Don't worry. I am sure I can find someone."

"But what will he be like? What . . . who . . . I can't just marry anybody . . . are you nuts?"

"Why not? Don't worry. I will find one. But why couldn't you just marry anyone?"

"Well, what is this person like? How do you know I will like him?"

"Wait a minute," I said. "Why does that matter? I thought you had no requirements and were into unconditional love. You said you wanted someone to like you just as you are. Now you are saying you have requirements for the person you want to marry. Are you saying you won't be unconditional with the man you like? You may not like something about him? That doesn't sound very unconditional to me. Sounds like you have some idea of what is okay with you and what is not, but you don't want this guy to have things he's looking for. That sounds like a double standard to me."

She got the point, yet she was kind of mad. She thought it was okay for her to have requirements on what she was looking for, but that if anyone else had requirements, they violated unconditional love. What a double standard, and also, what a fantasy!

The truth is that babies can do whatever they want, act like whatever they want, achieve little or nothing, and their mothers will love them to death. They are truly accepted unconditionally. But at about the end of the first year, things change. Parents begin to put boundaries on their behavior. They are required to meet standards and expectations. Some things they do are met with approval and other things are not. Life is not so "unconditional" as when they were born.

Life makes requirements on us; even God does that. God's *love* is unconditional, but his *approval* and what he is attracted to is very conditional. Some things he loves, and other things he hates. This is part of his nature, which he has passed on to us.

Now don't get me wrong. I am not saying that there is no such thing as unconditional love that looks past imperfections. That is the meaning of *agape*. It is the way that God loves us and the basis of any good relationship, especially marriage. But to make a relationship work and be enjoyable for both parties, there are things that matter to both people. You can't expect to slack off, behave poorly, neglect your chores, ignore your appearance, have crummy manners, be a bad listener, disregard people who are talking to you, or be uncompassionate, and think that people are just going to fawn all over you, as your mother would. Some things are attractive and make being around a person enjoyable and other things are not. I hope they are not as shallow as appearance, but they nevertheless exist for all of us, even the woman above.

Give up the fantasy that the opposite sex is supposed to somehow not be looking for someone who is attractive to him or her, whatever that means to each person. You have to realize that you too have things *you* deem attractive and things you do not. This is okay. I have talked about how those tastes can change. For instance, the more someone is open to all types of people, the more they find other things that are wonderful about a person, and they fall in love with those qualities.

But the lesson here is: *Have some of those qualities.* Be a person who is all of who God made you to be, and develop all you are. You do not have to be a beauty queen to attract someone, but chances are you will be more attractive if you are healthy and in shape, for sure. That speaks to a lot more than just being some false "ideal." It speaks to life, and how who God made you to be comes through more if you are healthy. The same is true for men and women. Either sex can't expect or demand someone he or she desires to just ignore unhealthy appearance, personal habits, or the way one lives, and coo over you like a mother does her newborn no matter what.

If you are in good physical shape, developing interests, engaged in hobbies, and performing service to humanity, you are more attractive than if you are a couch potato, not doing much about anything in life, and expecting that picture to knock some man or woman off his or her feet. Get real.

So, don't get in a huff that men and women are looking for things they find attractive. You are too, otherwise you would just get a mail-order date or spouse and be perfectly happy. At the same time, don't buy into Madison Ave.'s ideal and think you have to be that. It is amazing how women obsess over their appearance; half the time they are worrying about things only other women care about! Men could care less about half of those things.

Good men look for the natural beauty of the real person shining through, the sex appeal that comes from the radiance of a woman's personality, strength, humor, playfulness, virtue, and other things. It has little to do with being a physical 10. Healthy men look for a spark and an openness toward them that says "I like you and I am not mad at you for being a man."

While some men do look for the elusive 10s, you don't want those men anyway. They hide a lot of problems under their search for the ideal, perfect image of a woman. Let them go backstage at fashion shows and search for their ideal model there. Then they will find out that these women are not as ideal as the airbrush makes them look and that most of them need to gain twenty pounds. The other things I have listed don't diminish with age and can't be augmented with surgery. That is what good men are looking for—the attractiveness of a woman's real personhood, not some image. But for her real personhood to be revealed, it can't be hiding under a lot of health or personal problems.

And women do not need for a man to be CEO of a Fortune 500 company to be attractive. If they do, they are probably looking for some symbol of something missing in them. What they *do* need is a man who has a sense of power and a real sense of being strong, which only comes from character, being an initiator, and knowing what he wants, thinks, and believes. If his sense of passion and strength of who he is in relation to her comes through, she usually could care less about his list of achievements. His major achievement should be his unconflicted passion for her that comes from his character (see chapter 22, "Where Is the Testoserone?").

So, while you don't have to be ideal in every way, who you are *matters*. Do unto others as you would want them to do unto you! If you want your significant other to be attractive to you, then stop trying to *find* that person and focus on *becoming* that person. It is like looking for the job of your dreams. You prepare yourself to be "hireable." You "get yourself in shape."

When Lillie got serious about turning her dating life around, she faced the reality that she had let herself get out of shape and wasn't as attractive as her real, healthy self normally would be. So, she joined a program, and lost thirty pounds. She realized that being out of healthy shape was part of the stagnation she had allowed herself to slip into.

That is one example, but there are others. I have seen both men and women get serious about getting their entire personhood "into shape" as part of transforming their dating lives. They woke up from thinking that they were just somehow "entitled" to have someone like and want them, even when they were not being all that they were created to be. It is so exciting to see a person begin to care about all of his or her life and become well-rounded and more of a whole person. And if just a dating coach and people's friends and family like it and notice it, so will the "eligibles"!

So if you are ready for the hard part, don't do this by yourself. Submit yourself to the people who are committed to you and ask them. Ask them to honestly tell you what is not attractive about your:

- character
- habits
- personality
- spiritual life
- physical appearance
- fashion or lack thereof
- time or life management
- defenses

- interactions with the opposite sex
- health habits
- financial habits
- pursuit of life, career, dreams, and potential

It may be time for a "makeover." That is not a shallow pursuit but a call to be all that you were created to be, both on the inside and out. Solomon in the Song of Songs reflects the appreciation of physical attraction:

> *How beautiful you are, my darling!*
> *Oh, how beautiful!*
> *Your eyes are doves.*
>
> *How handsome you are, my lover!*
> *Oh, how charming!*
> *And our bed is verdant.*
> *(Song 1:15–16)*

Solomon goes into great detail throughout the Song of Songs about physical attraction and beauty as well as about character. And both Solomon and the apostle Peter uphold the value of character and inner beauty, even above outside attractiveness (see Prov. 31:30; 1 Peter 3:3–5). It is about the *total* package of a person. As you become more of who you were created to be, inside and out, you become more attractive.

This is a place also where people get hung up, especially in our society. *There is no absolute standard for what is beautiful.* To some it is one thing, to others it is something different. That is why there is someone for everyone. Your job is to be the best "you" God made you to be. Having worked with couples for many, many years, I can tell you that the common mistake is when people do not realize the attractiveness of their *personhood* and instead focus only on the outside.

Men, your initiative and assertiveness, blended with tenderness and empathy, plus a sense of humor put you way ahead of the crowd. And, get in shape, for a spare tire never turned any heads. But get in shape *inside*—be strong and compassionate. Learn how to listen, but don't be such a softy that she feels as if she can control you. That is death to passion for a healthy woman. She wants someone, as I hear often, who "won't let me get away with things."

Women, don't be controlling or smothering, because that registers in his mind as "motherly." Men are hard-wired to "leave their mothers and cleave." If you come across like a mother, he will leave and go find a woman who does *not* seek to control him. Instead, be open, independent, warm, and appreciate him without critical fault-finding, but not to the point of flattery or being giddy. He wants someone real. And that includes someone who is honest with him as well, even about where he is wrong. In the same way that women want someone who can stand up to them, good men want a woman who can be assertive without being controlling.

Above all, if you have some issue with men just because they are men, get over it. They do not want to be disliked just because they are men. They want that to be a plus! Many women's subtle disdain for men is a problem they never realize is sneaking out in unseen ways and keeping them stuck.

Both of you, men and women, be interesting and, as research shows, *funny*! Everyone has his or her own sense of humor, and it is different for all. Some are class clowns, and some are subtle. Some are dry, and some are comedic. It comes from inside you and what you see as funny. Attraction research shows that a sense of humor is always way up there as an important quality. And, remember, bad habits and anxiety quirks are always a turn off. So, work those out somewhere.

In the end, it is about being *real* and *genuine*. Be who you are, but make sure that who you are is quality! Would you want the person of your dreams wanting anyone less than quality? You don't want to be a ministry outreach for them! You want to be someone they feel as though they won the lottery to be out with. And to do that, you don't have to have surgery or put on a fake show. You just have to be healthy, strong, warm-hearted, open, and fulfilled in life. That will come through, and it is very sexy!

Picture the kind of person you want to date, and ask yourself: What kind of person would that person want to be with? It's your move.

28

Unleash Your Libido or Reel It In

Faith called in a panic. She was at a convention, and a few months into my coaching her. She was getting out there more and had experienced some growth, so attending this convention, where there would be many single men, had excited her. She did not anticipate it would scare her as well.

"There are so many guys here!" she said. "I am just freaking out, and I need some reassurance. I want to go to my room, order ten pizzas, watch TV, and hide. But another part of me wants to go see what is out there. Talk to me! HELP!"

We talked about why she was nervous and about getting her head right, lowering the risks, and having a good time. "Go back to the plan," I said, over and over. "This is about fun. No expectations. No list or requirements. Not looking for a husband. No proposals, just howdy-do. Have a good time and meet lots of them. Notice what you like, and so on."

It was a good talk. She got to the place where she actually looked forward to going to one of the gatherings.

Then I asked her a question: "What are you wearing?"

"Why?" she asked.

"Just wondering, what is it?"

"Well, nothing special. Just jeans and a shirt."

"What kind of shirt?" I asked. I was beginning to suspect something.

"Just a jersey kind of thing."

Hmm, I thought. "Hair?" I was getting suspicious.

"I just have it in a ponytail cause I am wearing a baseball hat," she said. "It is pretty casual around here."

"Okay, stop it," I said. "You are in jeans, a jersey, and a baseball hat, and you are going to meet guys?"

Now you have to understand something here. There is nothing wrong with what Faith was wearing. Many women can be very natural, attractive, and have appropriate sex appeal in that attire. But I knew Faith. I had seen this outfit on her. It did not allow anyone to even see what she was really like. It was more like a way to hide.

"Yes, it's just a casual atmosphere," she said. "What is wrong with that?"

"You're hiding, that's what. You're hiding behind your 'make myself look as little like a woman as possible, so I won't be rejected' strategy, and it's going to work. You are not going to be noticed. Why are you hiding?"

At first she balked, but the more we talked, she owned up to it. She had considered dressing differently, especially sans the cap, but when she had, she had gotten nervous. So, we explored that.

I asked her what she wanted, what she desired. And I asked her how she felt when she got in touch with her desires for a relationship with a man, for romance, for intimacy, for sex in marriage, and all of the good things God had put into her. As she talked about the things she desired, she felt herself coming alive, feeling more energy. But she was also *afraid*. She was afraid not only of rejection but also of the feelings themselves. She equated having the feelings and the desires with immorality. As a result of that thinking and fears of rejection, she had totally desexualized herself, and she was not attracting anyone.

"Get back in the dressing room right now!" I commanded. "Let your beautiful hair down, put on something that would at least identify you as a woman in a police line-up, and show a little sex appeal! No more hiding. God made you a woman, now go out there and be one!"

So she did. And the result was incredible. Not only did she scare herself into lots more growth, she also experienced a different dynamic with men. She began to—God forbid—*flirt.* Not coming on in some inappropriate way, but talking to good guys *as a woman* who said smart and funny things, was playful and made them enjoy themselves, was so at home with who she was that men felt comfortable being themselves around her. And they were. Soon she was getting noticed and dating regularly.

Unleash It

This is not an isolated situation. I had lunch recently with the pastoral staff of a large church at which I had led a seminar and with singles' leaders from other churches who had attended. We were talking about dating, and one of the women leaders said, "I was in a church that had a 'no-dating' spiritual teaching, and it was really weird. They said that you should not even kiss anyone you were serious about until marriage.

"One of my friends held to that, and she and her boyfriend, who was a main proponent of the teaching, were seen as so spiritual. She married him, but it has been a nightmare. Since they have been married, she found that all of his 'spiritual teaching' was covering the fact that he was hiding from sexual problems, insecurities, and a lot of weirdness. She is heartbroken and says, 'You know, I don't believe in sex before marriage, but I think if I had at least kissed him when we were engaged I would have instantly known he had some problems.'"

The point is not kissing or no kissing. It is much more serious than that. What that led to in our discussion was something very clear to these singles' leaders and something I see over and over as well. In the name of purity, chastity, and good morals, *singles have been desexualized*. They are often repressed beyond normal decency, and as a result they are in a "presexual" stage of development—what psychologists refer to as "latency." In other words, *out of a fear of sex, they have regressed to preadolescents, and they are feeling and acting like twelve-year-olds instead of adults who have gone through adolescence and figured all of that out*. Getting shut off from sexuality causes a shutdown of the dating process.

When there is such a negative emphasis on sexuality, people fear their sexuality and get so out of touch with it that the sexual dynamic disappears from expression in their personality. They no longer attract someone of the opposite sex because their God-given sexuality has been turned off. There is little "chemistry." They dress it away, they talk it away, they preach it away, and it goes away.

Others have another problem. With this teaching, many who already fear sexuality get more afraid. They bring their own fears to the situation because of past abuse, family dynamics, or hurt. So the teaching about how destructive sex is fits right in with their fears and experiences. They shut down even further, and instead of healing and embracing their sexuality, they see getting rid of it altogether as the "spiritual" thing to do.

Still others have a different problem. They have been *too* sexual in the past and have acted impulsively. They are in danger of acting out again and are probably sex or romance "addicts," so they adopt a rigid spirituality that "keeps the lid on." They are desperately afraid to feel sexual again, lest they act out. It would be like giving an alcoholic a smell of good wine. Watch out, because they have no self-control!

So repression causes two problems. On the one hand, some are repressed because they are out of touch. On the other hand, some are repressed because they are trying to hold it all back. Both of them make rigid rules to try to keep it all together. But scaring people does not bring about maturity or self-control (see Col. 2:23).

Keeping one's sexuality in an immature and unintegrated state makes it neither holy nor ready for real relationship. The idealization of being nonsexual as a symbol of spiritual maturity does not serve singles well. It hurts them in many ways. It keeps them out of what God designed as natural attraction, and it keeps sexuality disintegrated from the rest of their personhood. So when they do get into a relationship, it is not a part of the rest of them and has a life of its own. This gives way to acting out, loveless sex, fear, and dysfunction, among other things.

Sexuality needs to be integrated into one's personhood. It should be connected to all of who you are, and it should show up in real life, not be sent to a dungeon. Get in touch with your sexual desires and the fears you have about them. Talk to a counselor if you have had bad experiences and get those things healed. Dress in ways that do not hide your attractiveness, practice self-control, and do not act out your sexuality.

I do not advocate sexual acting out. I advocate sexual ownership as a part of who you are.

As one woman put it, "I had to unleash the beast within. I had totally cut myself off from my sexual feelings, and it was part of why I was not attracting anyone. When I got in touch with myself, things changed."

Another woman, Jenny, who is making great progress using these principles, had hardly dated in her "first thirty-two years," as she put it. Her mother had made her feel very guilty about her sexuality, and she had totally avoided it. At thirty-two, with no dating in her life, she came to me for coaching. One of the first things she had to see was that she was not attracting men because of this dynamic. It totally scared her. She recalled once in high school when a boy tried to kiss her goodnight and she freaked out, and that was just about the end of it for her.

Slowly she faced her sexuality, embraced it, and stopped dressing in ways that hid her attractiveness. She stopped shying away from interacting with men in any way that would make her seem feminine. Then she took the steps of meeting "five a week" and having no list of expectations. She began to come alive and worked on her fears. Slowly she inched back into being in touch with her sexuality. Here is what she wrote me just about her journey from being sexually shut down to coming back to life:

"Puberty hit me the summer between my freshman and sophomore years in high school; I started noticing boys on my soccer team as more than teammates. But as I became aware of my sexuality, I immediately became ashamed of my desires. They felt good and disgusting all at once.

"My mom subtly questioned my sexual orientation from time to time because I wasn't feminine enough, while my dad would look all googly-eyed at me when I felt pretty. I always thought he should be looking at my mom the way he looked at me. To be safe, I landed somewhere in the middle—female but not feminine. I cut off the whole part of my heart that would normally be alive with desires for dating, marriage, and intimacy (physically or emotionally) with a man. Getting close to a man scared the living daylights out of me. So, the idea of dating and marriage has been more frightening and distasteful than desirable to me for most of my life.

"Single life has felt much less risky and seemed nearly as much fun—that is, of course, until all my friends started dating and getting married. Then *my* heart began 'waking up' to desires for intimacy I'd never known before.

"As I watched Sonja and Andy [her friends] grow in their relationship, God showed me how my fear of intimacy had worked to deaden my heart to healthy longings for a love relationship with a man. I saw, too, how I'd let fear keep me from letting God heal and restore life to parts of my heart I'd hidden away at the age of fifteen. *I reached a point where I didn't/don't want to be dead anymore. As scary as it is to risk, I want to be fully alive!!*

"After Sonja and other friends who were working these principles had seen some success, I decided to 'get out there' and meet guys by signing on to a Christian online dating service. It took me about a month to finally get signed on and into communication. I literally was so nervous that for weeks I would go to the site, freak out, nearly throw up, and sign off before ever 'meeting' anyone.

"Eventually I worked up to communicating online, then talking on the phone, and even meeting one guy who flew down from New York. When my membership expired, I signed onto a different service. By the time that membership ran out, I hadn't found 'the love of my life' but the guy-meets-girl thing at least seemed normal.

"I'm actually dating . . . and I'm not running away!

"This is the cool part. In February, a friend of mine set me up with a guy she knew through work. I had overcome so much fear and was aware enough of my heart's desire that I could say, without hesitation, 'Yes, I would really like that.'"

"We met and had a great time, and we have been getting to know each other since. I still have fears about lots of things, but I'm not hiding. Instead, I'm being honest with myself and others, involving friends in the process, taking one day at a time, and paying attention to how I experience this man and how I feel when I am with him. I'm just trying to enjoy the process, trust God's principles, and let him take care of the risk management.

"I don't know where this relationship will end up, but that's okay. I'm 'practicing' this thing called dating and am glad to be doing so. It can be hard work. *It's worth it, though . . . to be fully alive, it's worth it.*"

I rejoiced at her story as it so illustrates what we have been talking about. She was "getting unstuck," by taking ownership of her issues and stepping out. Spiritual growth was becoming real and having fruit in her dating life.

Reel It In

Sometimes people have dating problems because of the opposite scenario. They are not out of touch with their sexuality. *Their sexuality is all they use in their dating.* They lead with their sexuality and hide the rest of themselves, just as Jenny hid her sexuality and femininity. They idealize sex, or at least embrace it as all of what a relationship is.

Men do this when they see women as sex objects and disregard the relational aspects of being a person and knowing a person. They see dating as a way to get married so they can finally legitimatize sex, and they are attracted to women solely on that basis. Disregarding character and also their own needs to learn how to relate on deeper levels, they set up themselves and the women they date for disaster.

In addition, many inappropriately engage in sexual expression in dating. Instead of focusing on real relationships, getting to know a person, embracing one's values, and being responsible as they get to know someone, they often have sex as part of the dating relationship. This is destructive on several levels.

First, it keeps them from seeing the real person. Sex is powerful, and it can hold two people together for a while when nothing else would. As a result, one or both are not realizing that there is nothing to this relationship other than the physical. So, as their bodies become one, they get attached at very hurtful soul levels. They think they are in love, but they are only in lust. In the end, they find out the truth, that the person they have been sleeping with is no one with whom they would want to spend the rest of their lives. Yet, they have given them all that they are physically.

Second, they further split love from their sexuality. If they are having sex, and yet they don't feel enough love to make a full commitment to the person, they give 100 percent of their body and less than 100 percent of the rest of themselves. By definition, their heart, soul, mind, and life are split from their bodies. They are disintegrated people, and it fragments their personhood. Then, later, when they do love someone with all of themselves, they often find that their sexuality is not connected to love, and they experience problems in that disconnected state. Sometimes the one they love cannot satisfy them—only a fantasy object can, since love and sex are split.

So, if you are having sex without a total commitment from the other person—and you know you have total commitment only when the other person says "I do" with a preacher there—then hold on to your body. Do not become one flesh until you have joined your lives together in marriage. If you do, you might end up marrying someone you really do not know, because the sex was good and got in the way of your knowing him or her. As Paul says,

> It is God's will that you should be sanctified: that you should avoid sexual immorality; that each of you should learn to control your own body in a way that is holy and honorable, not in passionate lust like the pagans, who do not know God; and that in this matter no one should wrong or take advantage of a brother or sister. The Lord will punish all those who commit such sins, as we told you and warned you before. For God did not call us to be impure, but to live a holy life. Therefore, anyone who rejects this instruction does not reject a human being but God, the very God, who gives you his Holy Spirit.
>
> (1 Thess. 4:3–8 TNIV)

Don't see this as God being some kind of cosmic killjoy. He is the one who invented sex. He wants you to have a great sex life with a mate. And to do that, he wants you to have it with love. So, see this as protective, as God means it to be. Embrace it as health.

There is one more important thing. Many women give themselves to a guy sexually as a way to have the guy like them. They feel that if they sleep with him, he will fall in love with them, and they will finally get the love they need. Nothing is farther from the truth. If a guy loves you, he will wait for you. In fact, you may not know whether he truly loves you if he doesn't have to wait for you. Sex may be the only reason he is around. And most times, they lose respect for you in the process and want to marry someone who is not so "easy."

In addition, you better find out if he has self-control before you marry him, not after. If he can't wait now, what guarantee do you have that he will be able to delay gratification after he is married? How do you know you can trust him? (Or vice versa if it is the woman who is pushing for sex.) Living out one's values and having self-control before marriage is a great way to see if someone has the character *for* marriage.

For men, sex confuses the issue because it keeps them from looking at who the woman is whom they are dating. The sex is so gratifying that the man fails to pay attention to the quality of the relationship itself apart from sex. He has no idea what she is really like to be with just as a person if there were no sex. It sets him up to be blinded by sex and to make bad choices in women. But if there is no sex, it forces him to look at the quality of the woman's character and the kind of relationship they have and to see if she is someone he really wants to be attached to.

So, find out if he or she truly loves you, or just your body. Find out if they truly have the character to live out the values they espouse. If not, be warned.

Work It Out

So, whether or not you need to get unrepressed or reeled in, do it to have the kind of dating life we are talking about here. Dating is a time of getting to know someone, and that includes the normal experience of sexual feelings and attraction. But, it is a time of getting to know who they are as a person, not hiding from that process by jumping into sex. Either extreme is a problem.

If you are too repressed or too loose with your sexuality, work it out. Get with a counselor, like Jenny did. Join a group, like others do. Find a good group of peers to talk it out with and work through it. Learn how God values sex and places high priority on it in marriage. Heal from past sexual problems or even abuse, if that has happened to you. Sometimes, if you have been treated like an object, you either lose touch with your sexuality or allow others to continue to use you now. Get healing for that through good counseling.

If you have been sexually active in dating, you can receive God's forgiveness and be totally cleansed from guilt and failure. Remember, God has promised to forgive all things and make it all new. With God, you truly can start over, and from this day forward, be as clean and pure as snow. Just ask God to forgive you, cleanse you, and start over. If you do, dating will be a lot clearer.

Either way, integrate sex with all of you, including your values. Then, as a whole person, you will be much more in position to find a date worth keeping.

29

Do You Have to Get Married?—Dating Is Not for the Lonely

My friend Michael was obsessed with finding a wife. This search consumed much of his energy and focus. He saw his intense desire for marriage as a healthy, God-given one, thinking that, as Proverbs says, "he who finds a wife finds what is good and receives favor from the LORD" (Prov. 18:22).

But his obsession was having a threefold effect in his life. First, it was ruining his dating life. He was having no fun at all and going on fewer and fewer dates. He evaluated each woman he dated as a "prospect" for marriage. He could not see a woman as someone to get to know, and he was lost in looking for someone who didn't exist.

Second, he was not growing and changing into the person he needed to be, both to find the right one and to be the right one for someone else. Since his focus was entirely on finding "her," he was ignoring the things in his own life he needed to change and the places where he needed to grow. He was stuck as a person and did not know it. He just felt as if he needed to "find the right one."

Third, he was not growing spiritually. Getting married had become his idol. That desire had overshadowed his contentment and enjoyment of his relationship with God and the other wonderful blessings God had given him in life, including friends, his work, and his passions. He had a full life but felt empty.

Then one day something unusual happened. You may not believe this, but it's true. One Sunday he went to visit a church he had never been to. After the service, when he was standing in the sanctuary, an older gentleman walked up to him, introduced himself, and said, "God spoke to me about you. I would like to share with you what he said."

Michael didn't know what to do, so he said, "Okay, give me your phone number." The man gave it to him, and Michael said he would call him.

When he got home, Michael called his friend Will, who went to that church, and told him what had happened.

"What's the guy's name?" Will asked.

Michael told him.

"Whatever you think about this, you have to go. This guy doesn't do that often, but when he does, people go out of their way to listen. He has a reputation for being right about what he prophesies. We take him very, very seriously. Listen to what he tells you."

Michael was surprised, as he'd never experienced anything like this before. But he trusted his friend, so he called the man and met with him.

"Here is what I heard God say to you," said the old gentleman. "Stop looking for a wife. You will know it when she comes along."

Michael was shocked. How did this man know about his intense pursuit? What did it mean that he would know when she came along? He had more questions than he had answers, but the man said that he was sorry, he had no more than what he had given him. With that, he left.

This encounter was life-changing. My friend stopped looking for a wife. He deepened his relationship with God, worked on his life, and began dating without the obsessive pursuit. He enjoyed dating again. In that next year he went through deep spiritual changes, personal changes, and growth he never would have gone through if he hadn't given up his idol. And you can probably guess the rest of the story—when she came along, he was able to recognize her. Now they are happily married, and she was a lot different from the types he had looked for before his strange encounter.

Now, lest you take from this the wrong lesson—that is, "See, I don't have to do anything, God will bring me a spouse"—I should tell you that there is more to this story than that. Michael went into the process I'm talking about in this book. He gave up dating as a spouse hunt and began seeing it as an enjoyable activity. He learned about himself and other people. He deepened his life with God. He focused on having a balanced life full of contentment and activities. He faced issues that God was bringing up in his life that needed to be faced. He worked the program.

The woman whom he married he saw at church, and he actively pursued getting a chance to meet her against all obstacles. God did not just have her walk up to him and say, "Here I am, the one God told you about." He had to work hard to get an opening to meet her. He had to pursue her. He had to "sow" in order to "reap." He had to be active. (See chapter 22, "Where Is the Testosterone?") So, do not make the mistake of thinking that if God is active in your life, you don't have to be. It is both.

If the only way you are active is in obsessing over finding a mate, then you are probably not ready to find one. Here are some things to think about:

- *Are you content with your life?* If not, then it is not time for marriage. Marriage or a significant relationship is about two healthy, content people coming together, and the "two becoming one." If they are not "whole" people, you don't have two becoming one. You have a half of a person joining another half of a person, hoping to find wholeness. Remember that one half times one half equals one fourth. You will end up worse than when you started if you do not get a whole life first.

- *Are you seeking a relationship to end loneliness?* If you are, it won't. Cure your loneliness first. You must have a full heart to bring to a relationship, not an empty one. Get your relational needs met with a good community of friends. Otherwise, you are going to choose a mate out of dependency and need. If you do that, your judgment is going to be clouded by your needs, and you are more likely to choose badly.

- *What are you expecting marriage to provide for you?* If you think that it will make you happy when you are not, you are wrong. Unhappy people who get married create unhappy marriages. If you think it will cure your depression or emptiness, it won't. Depression and emptiness are conditions that need counseling, therapy, and spiritual growth. Work on those first, and then worry about getting married. Marriage will only complicate those issues. My advice is the same for things such as desire for security, fear, bad feelings about yourself, and feeling unloved. Work on those things first, then worry about marriage when you no longer need marriage to make up for those things.

- *Do you see marriage as a romantic fantasy or some other kind of unending bliss?* If so, you must get real about marriage. Marriage is a commitment between two imperfect people to love and sacrifice for each other and build something good. So take a hard look at those words—*"commitment, two, imperfect, love, sacrifice,* and *build."* They all require suffering, effort, delay of gratification, and other painful, character-building experiences. The fruit of those experiences can be very, very good. When love is built, it is a very good thing. But it requires work, and it is important you have a realistic view going into it.

- *Do you think that marriage is going to make your life significantly "better"?* While marriage can indeed make many things "better," it should not be seen as the way to make your *life* better. If something in your life is not good, fix it. Find a good life as a single. Make it an awesome life. The only kind of person anyone would want to marry anyway is someone with a good life. No one wants to be someone's "solution" for a life that's not working.

- *Do you want to get married to prove you are okay?* Sometimes people see marriage as a way of proving that they are desirable, that they fit into the rest of society. Or they seek marriage for some other external measure, such as being in with the "in crowd" or finally making their family happy. Marriage is not going to make you feel "okay," nor is it going to make you feel as if you measure up or fit in. Marriage is not a solution. It is a decision to change your state of existence, from single to married, and a lot of other things that go with that. But it doesn't solve problems that need their own solutions.

The bottom line is this: If you "have to get married" to feel good, have a full life, feel content, have a purpose, or fulfill any other reason, you better take a hard look at that. Get a full life first. Get healed first. Get your loneliness cured first. In short, learn how to have a full life as a single person. The best preparation for marriage is to become a whole, healthy person who does not need to get married. Then you can marry for the right reasons—not because you "need" to but because you "desire" to, and because it is the wise, right, timely, and God-ordained thing to do.

The best mates, and the most attractive singles, are the healthy ones with a full life that someone would want to join. No one wants to be a rescue mission for someone else, meaning that you need someone to marry you to make your life okay. How attractive do you think that is?

So, this is the great paradox. To not need marriage might mean you have a much greater chance of getting married. Lose your idol to receive what God has for you. "Seek first his kingdom and his righteousness, and all these things will be given to you as well" (Matt. 6:33).

30

Turn Off the Autopilot and Drive

Tricia was disappointed with her dating life. To me it was clear why. What was not clear was why it wasn't clear to her. Her complaint was that "guys just have a problem with commitment." My view was that she had a pattern of attracting guys who have a problem with commitment.

Here is what she would do. She would meet a guy she liked, and they would go out. Since she was very attractive, he would instantly like her and obsessively go after her. Since she defined herself by what men thought of her, she fed on the attention, and it tapped into her need to be pursued. She did not notice that it was a lot, very quickly. She bought it. They became too close too quickly, giving up way too many boundaries. She could see herself "falling for him" much too fast, but the bliss and excitement got in the way of worrying about anything.

When, after a few months, she started falling in love, something would happen. The guy would slowly back off, not call as much, and make excuses about "all the work he had to do." She would feel sad, ignored, and abandoned. At first she would pout, then she would protest his behavior more directly. He would see this as her being another "controlling girlfriend" and protest back. She would give in because she wanted him, but she was not happy.

Soon, he would be gone, saying, "I really like you, but I don't think I am in love with you." She had heard this many times. Then she would conclude, "Guys are just afraid of commitment."

To me, her pattern was clear and easy to change. If she could see it, she could fix it. My job was to get her to see that her failed relationships with men were no random occurrence, but something she was setting up and participating in, not something that was "happening to her." If she could see her tendency in the beginning of a relationship to adapt way too much to someone she liked, she could maintain her boundaries in ways that would not have smothered the guy, even though he was "asking for it."

Since she was the type who fused with men who had no boundaries, she attracted them. It was magnetic. And such men were going to do what most men with poor boundaries do: come on strong at the start and then later create distance to avoid being smothered or controlled. If she could keep a healthy, structured life from the start, not only would the outcome be different, but also she *would attract a whole different kind of man*. If she had boundaries, she would more likely attract a man with boundaries.

I have no way of explaining how the chemistry of initial attraction works, except that people with complimentary dynamics seem to attract each other. Don't ask me how, but they do. The daughter of the alcoholic can pick out the alcoholic in a room full of healthy men just by feeling attracted to him. And the alcoholic seems to hone in on the codependent in a room full of women. The adaptive woman can find the controlling man without giving him a psychological test. The only test she needs is the butterflies in her stomach and her energy level going up.

After people work through their patterns, their unhealthy attractions change, and in fact, disappear. How? There are many complicated reasons, but one of them is that health seems to be an acquired taste. When people develop healthy patterns, they don't go back. A good analogy may be that of a junk-food junkie: Once he changes his eating habits, he loses his taste for greasy fast food. He truly wants his steamed veggies.

Work through your issues, and the control freak that used to turn your head will make you sick to your stomach. So, how do you do that? Learn your pattern so you can avoid repeating it, follow the suggestions in the "Get Healthy" chapter (chapter 25), and use your friends to help. Here are some examples of unhealthy patterns:

1. You feel a strong attraction to someone and give up everything to pursue him instead of staying connected to the rest of your life.

2. When you like someone, you slowly avoid speaking your mind or asserting yourself. You adapt to whatever she wants.

3. You feel attracted to someone and instead of actively pursuing him, you lose your initiative. You are too shy, and you pull back instead of actively being yourself "toward" them.

4. You find someone you like, but if there is one slight feeling of rejection, such as if she has other plans or one date doesn't go well, you disappear.

5. You start dating someone you like, but the more you go out with him and get close, the more you find little things "wrong" with him. You use those things as an excuse to blow him off.

6. You begin dating someone and give up too many physical boundaries too quickly.

7. You like someone a lot until he likes you, and then for some reason, he is not attractive anymore.

8. You see many reasons why someone is not "right" for you until she doesn't want you, and then she looks wonderful.

9. You fall for someone until she protests some things and then you see her as a nag, and you look for someone who is "easier."

10. You go out a few times and worry that this looks too "serious," so you move away. You feel too responsible for the other person. You feel as though it's not okay to date without a commitment, so you keep your distance or bail out too soon.

11. You stay in a relationship that is not a relationship, but it's comfortable for both of you. You know it's not what you want, but it's "something to do" instead of being alone. You're stuck in a pseudo-friend-pseudo-dating relationship.

12. You are attracted to an "unattainable." She may be unattainable because of age, geographical distance, social barriers, or some other reason, but you are only able to love what you can't have.

13. You find one person you like and give up dating others, going from one to another, instead of dating a lot of people at once. So, over time, you date very few people. Your numbers are "low."

14. When the person you are dating shows character flaws that should signal you to move on, you interpret those signals as something wrong with you. You try to please that person into loving you. For example, she is emotionally detached or not responsive, and you try to please her to get her to love you.

These are only a few of the available "patterns." All of them have fixed kinds of dysfunction between personality attributes of people that are a match. So, that is why there are fireworks, attractions, and predictable games. The trick is to recognize a pattern and to stop it. When a relationship starts to feel familiar to you, that's a sign you've been there before.

The next step is to do something *different* from what your autopilot is programmed to do. Start to do the healthy thing where normally you would do the unhealthy thing, over and over again. Then you are on your way to changing the pattern and growing.

Sandy had a pattern. She would fall for a guy and have a great beginning, and then he would become detached. At that point, she would try to draw him closer, using a variety of tactics. When she felt his emotional unavailability and his moving away, she would become heartsick and would long for him desperately. When she told me about this pattern, I told her to keep a journal of her dates and to write down *how she felt when she was with him.*

At first, she talked about her attraction as "love." She felt as though she "loved him." She desired him and loved being "with" him. But the more we talked about it and unraveled it, what she was calling "love" was really unmet longing. She was lonely. There was nothing truly satisfying about being with him. I asked her to tune into exactly how she felt both on their dates and after their dates. The more she did, the more she got the noise of "wanting him" out of her head and began to see exactly what it was like to be with him. *It was a lonely experience.* To be with this guy was to be alone, period. That is who he was.

When she understood that, then instead of responding on autopilot to his detachment by diligently seeking his unattainable heart, she took control. She did not chase him to get him to love her more, something of which he was incapable. She asked herself the question: "Do I really want someone with whom I feel alone? Is that what I desire? Do I want to spend time with someone and feel as if I am by myself? Do I want to feel rejected when I am trying to love someone?" The obvious answer was no. She called him and told him it was over.

Within months, she was attracted to another kind of man altogether, and now she is married to a very emotionally available guy. If she had not seen her pattern, turned off the autopilot, and taken control of the steering wheel, she would still be there. Figure out your patterns that have led nowhere and stop them. Take control of the wheel, in all stages of dating.

1. *Initiating.* What do you do automatically? Shy away? Go into the background? Overpower someone? Wait for him or her to decode the combination to open the "safe" and break through? Make an initial effort, and then shy away after the slightest obstacle? You will continue to get the same results if you continue your pattern.

2. *Going out.* Do you adapt? Come on too strong? Play as if you are not interested and never get a call back? Are you emotionally unavailable? Too gushy? Too available? Do you talk about having babies before the salad comes? Overlook problems because you like the person or are desperate? Talk about your exes?

3. *Going out on a second date and beyond.* Do you give too much too quickly? Shy away? Make it too serious instead of going out for fun? Read too much into it? Give up other dates too quickly? Fail to recognize that this is the type you have failed with before?

4. *Dating formally.* Do you hang on too long when you should be gone? Not stand up against destructive patterns? Settle for something you really don't want? Fear commitment? Don't pay attention to your doubts and that "still small voice"?

Find the automatic patterns working against you and change them. If you write a different script, you will have a different outcome. But if you continue to act out the same old one, you'll see only reruns of your old relationships. Take charge.

Part 4

Stay Focused on What's Important

31

Will This Friendship Ever Heat Up?

You have been friends for a long time. The relationship has remained platonic and has not morphed into more. Yet, you love this person and enjoy his or her company, and you think that he or she is the kind of person you would like to be in a more serious relationship with. Could it turn into more? Should it?

This dilemma has no right or wrong answer, but I know, from working with many people, that many individual situations have different problems, answers, and outcomes. Here are some thoughts to help you to think about whether the friendship you are in with a member of the opposite sex will ever heat up.

Friendship Is Good

Friendship is the way all dating should begin anyhow. Even if you are very attracted to a person, you should not jump immediately into romance or coupling overtones. Dating is about getting to know a person, sharing, talking, doing things together, and exploring spiritual matters—and that is what friends do. So, in a sense, every relationship should begin there. If you are there, this is not necessarily a "problem."

Friendships Can Progress into Something More

From "friends," relationships sometimes grow into "more than friends." Whatever term one places on this transition, another dynamic enters. Different aspects of the heart and different kinds of God-created love come into play. Sometimes, as two people get to know each other, they naturally progress to a qualitatively different kind of love as a result of all good things coming together. When this happens well, it is natural and reciprocated. Most times, however, it does not happen on an exact parallel schedule. One person is often a little ahead of the other, but they are on the same track.

Three Reasons Things Might Not Progress (and What to Do about Them)

When this does not happen naturally, there may be three reasons why the friendship is not progressing into something more. One, the friendship could be something more, but things are standing in the way. Two, one person is progressing toward a love relationship and the other is not. Three, the friendship will always be a friendship. Let's take a look at those three reasons.

1. You've never taken the blinders off.

In the first instance, if you are in a friendship that is not progressing after you have tried all there is to try, at some point ask "Why?" Is it because the two of you have never taken the blinders off and taken a look at each other in "that way"? Is it because both of you have come from some other relationship and are playing it safe with each other? Is it time to talk about it and ask, "Have you ever wondered why we have never dated?"

You might find out that there is no good reason why the friendship is not moving toward a love relationship and that when you have the conversation, both of you wake up. Women have told me,

"He was there all along, and I never realized it because he was my best friend." When they finally opened themselves up to the option, the relationship progressed.

You might also find out that there are problems that have to be resolved, such as one person or the other may need to grow in some way. Or, he may be the old boyfriend of a friend of yours, and you never looked at him that way, or she may live in a different state or be a few years older than you. There are many others.

2. Only one person wants it to progress.

In the second instance, if only one person is falling in love, you have to find out why. Is the friendship not progressing to a love relationship because it's not going to progress? Is it not progressing because the other one does not know you are falling in love? Does he or she need to be invited to look at your relationship in that way? Is he or she frightened? Some very good love relationships began as friends and one person had to nurture the other one into a different kind of relationship because the other one was afraid of something and that fear had to be worked through. It took a lot of patience and time.

The key to remember, though, is if you are "wanting more" and it is not happening, at some point you must give up and move on. Do not stay stuck waiting for your friend to fall in love with you if there is no reason to think it will ever happen. Get on with it. Enjoy your friend, but don't park your hopes there for life.

3. It's just a friendship.

In the third instance, accept that this is a friendship. There is no rule that says friends ought to be able to make a friendship into something more and morph their brotherly/sisterly love into something romantic. If it's not there, great. That's a good thing. Don't try to make it something it's not. You need good friends! Don't mess it up by trying to make it more.

A Warning

Here is a big warning: If your dating life is not working and you are using some friendship that is never going to be more than friendship to enable you to stay stuck, stop it. If the two of you lean on each other to deal with your lack of a dating life, and sometimes you even venture into pseudo-romantic areas, but you both know you are not serious, stop it. Stop that crutch-like behavior and work on learning how to walk. It is not healthy, and it is not getting you further down the road where you want to be.

This does not mean that your friends should not meet your relational needs and be your primary support system. What I am talking about here is a sloppy regressive friendship that both of you lean on because you are not doing anything about what you truly want. That is very different from a friendship that is pushing you toward what you want and helping you grow so that you get there. Make your friendship one that makes you grow, take risks, and step out, not one that enables you to stay stuck because you have someone to hang out with. That is not helpful to either one of you.

32

Beauty Is Only Skin Deep, but Character Goes All the Way to the Bone

Do I really need to open with a story that illustrates the point of this chapter? I doubt it. You are probably walking around with stories in your head. Here is the formula I want you to get:

While you might be attracted to someone's "outsides," what you will experience over the long haul is their "insides."

In other words, many things we can readily see on the outside of a person are "beautiful" to us humans. Think of some that might draw you to a certain person:

- physical appearance
- intellect
- charm
- humor

- achievements
- people skills
- accomplishments
- talents
- style
- manners
- status

- degrees
- career
- tastes
- spiritual appearance
- economic standing
- power
- fame

These things might initially attract you—and even create excitement. Many of them are wonderful things. Beauty is attractive. Brains are interesting, as are someone's accomplishments, career, and education. Learning about people and the fascinating things they have done all make for fun and interesting conversation and interaction. A person who has achieved power in business, politics, entertainment, and education can be fascinating. Hearing the story of what people do and how they do it, and their special talents that got them where they are can be fun—fun, fascinating, attractive, interesting, sexy. This is all well and good, and it is part of getting interested in a person. People are awesome!

But getting interested in someone and *enjoying him or her in the long haul* are two entirely different things. The only things that last are in a person's *character*. Or, I should say the only thing that makes a relationship able to last is a person's character. You cannot "experience" someone's advanced degrees, for example. You can only experience *your* admiration for them and be attracted to that quality. But the power of that wears off. Hear that again: The power of all that will wear off. But, someone's *insides*, their character, their makeup is what you are going to experience in a relationship, long term. And, past a date or two, that is what you should be looking at very, very hard.

We have said "go out" with almost anyone. Be interested when interest is called for. But to "desire," to "want," to "open up your heart," and beyond that, "to give yourself" or "make a commitment," are things that should *only* be done with someone of good character.

When I talked about getting rid of your list of requirements, I was referring to dating and getting to know someone. Ditching the list of prerequisites is for learning and finding out who someone is, as well as who you are. It is for discovering that you might like some things you didn't know you liked and that some other things you thought were important are really not. It is for shopping.

But here is the time to draw up that list of requirements: *when you are thinking about involving your heart with someone.* At this point, you had better have strong requirements, and they should not relate to body type, profession, height or weight, hobbies, or things like that. The requirements should concern character.

Here are some things to look at:

- Can the person connect emotionally? Is she present with you? Do you feel heard, listened to, and like you are with someone when you are with her, as opposed to feeling alone?
- Does the person allow freedom, separateness, and your own choices to be okay? Or, does he try to control you, punish your freedom or independence, or not respect your choices?
- Does the person respect your limits and your no?
- Can he "go your way" as well as want his own way? Is he selfish or self-centered? Can he be as concerned about the wishes of others as he is about his own?
- Does she possess self-control and discipline? Or is she impulsive or irresponsible?
- Is he a perfectionist? Does he require you to be "ideal" instead of allowing you to be real and have imperfections? Does he act as if he "has it all together"? Does he seek his "ideal self" more than being "real?"
- Is she driven, or is she able to enjoy life and relationship?
- Does he face his pain, weaknesses, and problems? Does he confess when wrong and ask for forgiveness? Does he forgive others and accept his "bad parts"? Or is he condemning and judgmental?
- Does she have a set of passions, pursuits, and interests? Or does she just adapt to the flavor of the day and drift in life? Does she give herself to anything?

- Does he serve in some capacity and deny himself for others?
- Is she comfortable with her sexuality? Is she prudish? Does she act out sexually and have poor sexual limits? Does she push you for sex?
- Is he prideful or arrogant? Does he seem to think he is superior to others? Or does he feel inferior to the degree that he backs away from life?
- Is she too tied to her parents, even as an adult? Is she getting inappropriate help from parents? Does she still try to please one of her parents? Has she grown up?
- Does he respect authority? Can he submit to it?
- Can she take control and stand up to things? Can she say no and stick with it, even when someone does not like it?
- Can he take confrontation? Is he defensive? Can he hear complaints about himself and change his behavior when it is hurtful to someone?
- Can she be honest and assertive about what she wants?
- Is he trustworthy and loyal? Does he have zero deception? Does he have integrity in all he does?
- Does she blame others or see herself as a "victim"?
- Does he lie? Or can you trust him to always tell the truth?
- Is she growing in life and spiritually?
- Does his spiritual commitment have a life of its own? Or do you have to push it?
- Does she submit to God and obey him? Or is she her own "god"?
- Has he faced his "issues" and come to grips with whatever is in his past?
- Does she confront you and tell you when you are wrong or she doesn't like something? Is it with anger? Or is it with love?
- Does he have an emotional problem he hasn't faced? Is he easily angered?
- Is she religious or spiritual? Is her faith life a rigid one of rules, or is it about relationship and reality?
- What personal habits indicate character issues to you?

- What is her relationship history? If it is problematic, has she dealt with it in counseling, or are you the next victim?
- Does he communicate, or does he shut down? Does he face conflict and work it through with you? Does he use bad tactics like "put-downs" or sarcasm?
- Does she withdraw or does she seek you when something is wrong?
- Is he addicted? Envious? Jealous? Petty? Bitter? Resentful? Divisive or into cliques? Is he a social or status "climber"?
- Does she have empathy and concern for the hurting, weak, or less fortunate?
- Does he have long-term good friends?

I know, this is tedious stuff. But so is living with someone who has serious character issues. Remember, whatever this person is like, if it is a character issue, it is not going to change without that person admitting her problem and getting significant help. You are not going to change her, other than by not giving in to her problem and becoming an impetus for her to get help. You should count on getting what you see until she sees her problem and faces it.

This is not rocket science. Listen to your gut, your feelings, and your senses. As Hebrews 5:14 says, mature people use their senses to discern good things from bad. Listen to your feelings and what it is like to be "with" this person, apart from his attraction, charm, and "pull." "Experience your experience" of being with the person or in a relationship. This is what you will have long term—not the adoration, admiration, or infatuation of whatever you are idealizing. At some point, get down to who that person truly is.

As you look at these things, hold on to your heart and commitment until he or she is proven good. Here is a good formula from *Safe People*, a book I coauthored with John Townsend. People who are good for you are going to have a threefold effect over time:

1. *You end up closer to God.* This person does not take you away from God. This does not mean that he sees himself as a spiritual giant. It means that he shows you more of who

God is—God's love and God's nature—as a result of your relationship. He lives God's ways, and you can experience God together.

2. *You end up closer to others.* You are a more relational person and grow in your capacity to relate to others. You trust more, not less. You are more open, not shut down or kidnapped to just this relationship. You have grown in your relational capacities as a fruit of being with this person.

3. *You become more of yourself.* Instead of a person causing you to lose parts of yourself to be around her, the relationship helps you find more of who God created you to be. You expand, grow, stretch, and become a better and more whole "you," not less of you.

So, hold on to your heart in dating. Learn, experience, and have fun. Only give your heart to someone who deserves it. It is a precious commodity. As Jesus, says, "Do not give dogs what is sacred; do not throw your pearls to pigs" (Matt. 7:6). They will trample your treasures under their feet.

Good people do the opposite. They are a "safe deposit box" for the treasures of your heart. Only store them there, with good characters to whom you can truly trust your treasures. If you do that, not only will your treasures be safe, but their value will grow. That is the person you are looking for, the one to whom you can give your heart. Until then, have fun, but hold on!

33

Seven Extra Hints

As you begin to work through the steps contained in this book, you may encounter a few unanticipated dynamics—fears, obstacles, or challenges that could derail your progress. I want to walk through a few of these dynamics, unrelated as they are, because they are important to me, and I want you to be ready to address them, if and when they appear.

Move Beyond the Fear of Being Branded

One of the things I often hear from people, especially in Christian communities, is that they do not want to "just date" because they fear that if they do go out with someone, they will immediately be branded "as a couple." They fear that once they go out with someone, even casually, no one else will ask them out. So, paradoxically, they don't date, in order to date. Sounds a little self-defeating, don't you think?

And that is the result. For the most part, those with this mentality remain stagnant, as do the social circles that foster such a mentality.

There are two things you can do to address this problem. First, get over it. Move beyond the fear of being branded. Don't allow the views of other people to dictate how you live your life. If they do not have anything better to do than talk about your dating life, let them do that. As you date and continue to go out with other people, they will eventually realize that you are not a couple.

Second, if you are a member of a group that fosters this, do what you can to change the culture. Speak up! Voice your opinion that two people spending time together as friends and getting to know each other is not the same thing as a serious relationship. No one should expect a wedding invitation any time soon! Do what you can to bring dating back in style.

Move beyond the Fear of Hurting Someone

When people date, one person sometimes has more interest in the relationship than the other. At some point, the one with less interest realizes that the relationship is not going to progress beyond friendship and that it's time to initiate "the talk." Many people are so afraid of hurting someone who's grown attached to them that they avoid dating altogether.

The best way to address this is to be honest all along the way. Do not deceive someone or act as though you are more interested than you are. Such behavior raises the other person's expectations too high, too quickly. Probably most singles are guilty of this at some time or another because it's easy to do, especially at the beginning of a dating relationship. It's also important to remember that if you have been honest and clear, you are not responsible for the other person's feelings. He or she is an adult and freely chooses to be in the dating arena. However, that does not mean that you are free to do whatever you want, and then blame the other person for the results. As Jesus taught, treat others the way you want to be treated.

Dating is a period of getting to know someone and then figuring out what you want to do with what you discover about each other. There is *certain* risk, not theoretical risk. That is the nature of dating itself. When you date, you engage in an activity that includes the risk of being rejected. And the person you date has agreed to take that risk, just as you have. He or she is free to decide not to pursue the relationship with you as well. The risk is equally shared and part of being an adult.

As a result, people sometimes get hurt. If that happens, it is a disappointment and it involves grief and sadness. All of us must deal with disappointment in life; no one is exempt. Sad as it is, deciding you do not want to pursue a relationship with someone is not "harmful," but it may cause hurt. Harm and hurt are different. You inflict harm when you do something deceptive or something that causes people to lose faith in relationships or in people. Deciding that you do not want to move forward in a relationship, in and of itself, does not cause injurious harm, but it is a hurt to the other person that causes sadness. If the other person does feel harmed or injured, he or she may have other hurts from the past and other relationships that your breakup is magnifying. You did not cause those by breaking up. Just be kind and affirming, but also clear and honest.

Date Adults Only

If you are considering whether or not to get more serious in a relationship, make sure the person you are dating is an emotionally independent adult. Pay attention to the warning signs that indicate the person is too dependent on Mommy and/or Daddy. Date adults only. An adult is someone who has "left home" and draws emotional and spiritual support primarily from an adult community, not from parents. If the person you are dating appears to be inappropriately supported by parents, that's a warning sign. It doesn't mean support is bad, it just means that it should be appropriate. Adults should not be overly dependent on parents for finances, sustenance, decision making, guidance, approval, spirituality, or other things. If you find yourself in a relationship with someone who has not left home emotionally, you are dating a teenager and not an adult. Be careful.

First Be Safe

The bulk of this book is about meeting new people. This means you do not always know a lot about the people you meet. Therefore, it's important to be careful and practice safe dating.

Most of safe dating is simply common sense. Just as you would not give a stranger on the street access to your personal life, don't leave yourself unprotected with the dates you do not yet know a lot about. For example, if you meet someone through a dating service, be careful about disclosing too much information too soon.

This principle applies to dates from other sources as well. When friends introduce you to someone, they may not know what kind of person he or she is in the context of dating. They may know that he is a nice guy at work, but sometimes relationships bring out a whole other side of people not evident at work, in church, or other contexts of life. Remember, you really don't know this person.

It's not my intention to scare you, but it's important to remember that meeting someone new means you don't know him or her. That is also the good thing about dating: You get to know someone new and something wonderful may be in store for you. But, just in case that is not the outcome, be careful until you really know who this person is.

Use caution when meeting someone you don't know well, or the person who introduced you does not know well. Meet in public places or with friends. If you use a dating service, research the service's screening practices, safety policies, and/or suggestions. Read books on online dating that offer additional guidance.

Make sure that you know someone pretty well before agreeing to be alone or before giving that person access to information that could prove dangerous such as where you live, home phone number, and places where you can be found regularly. If possible, give either your cell phone number or your work number and a good time to call. Guard your home number from someone you do not yet know. Or, you could set up a free email address just for giving to dates, aside from your regular email that you want to keep for a long time and thus need to protect.

No matter how a person comes across or what you may assume about him or her, you just don't know. Don't allow yourself to assume that someone is okay just because he or she is connected to so and so, or because he looks successful, goes to a certain church, or works with the friend of a friend.

Remember, it's great to meet new people. Just be wise and cautious as you do.

Weigh the Friends Factor

Another dynamic to look for in someone you are getting to know is the nature of his or her friendships. Does this person have any? Are the friendships long term? Are the friendships with men and women? What is the nature of their community and support system? Is he or she "rooted and grounded," as the Bible says, in a good community?

Having long-term friends with whom one "does life" is a good sign. It is not everything, but it is something. A person who does not have long-term friendships and who is not rooted in a community should raise a big warning sign in your mind. I would say even a big stop sign. I would be hard pressed to think of an occasion where trusting a person with no long-term friends would make sense. You might end up instantly being this person's whole community. This is not a good thing. Gain some insight about the person from the kinds of friendships he or she has. Do the friendships exist, and what kind of friends are they? That can tell you a lot.

Leave Your Self-image Somewhere Else

In a recent seminar I taught, a single man said he did not like to date because he was afraid of being turned down or rejected. I said, "I certainly hope you *do* get turned down and rejected! A lot! Being turned down means you are asking out a lot of women, and the numbers are such that you *will* get turned down for a variety of reasons. But, if you are asking a lot of women, you certainly have better chances of doing well."

Expect rejection. It is part of the game. Don't give a potential date the power to decide for you whether you are lovable, likable, or desirable. Get the love and validation that you need from your friends, from your spiritual community, and from God. Develop the security you need, and from that place, go out into the dating arena. When you get turned down, you can go laugh about it with your friends and go for it again.

Don't allow getting turned down to be anything except a learning experience and evidence that you tried. If there is a reason you got turned down that you could change, such as your coming on too strong or some other personal trait, learn from that and go forward. Either way, don't let it affect you. Get your personal validation somewhere else. Consider dating from the perspective of a soldier in a war. (I hope it isn't that adversarial, so forgive me the metaphor!) You get your support from the ones on your side, and then you go out to battle and come back to get your support again. Lick your wounds and get back in there.

Above All, Have Fun!

Remember, dating is not supposed to make your life miserable. Dating is about growing—spiritually, personally, relationally—and having some great experiences. Don't let dating get you down, and don't put too much stock in any one date or any one person. There are a few billion more out there. Decide in advance to have a good time in this great adventure. If you end up getting married as a result, this is the only time you will ever have to just date. Enjoy!

A Final Heart to Heart from Your Coach

I just received a wonderful email from a couple who found each other and were married as a result of working the program about which you have just read. It was so cool to hear about the incredible partnership they are enjoying and to remember the "dating despair" they felt at one time. As a psychologist, I find it fun to watch someone go from being in the desert to finding their own promised land.

This couple tasted a true fairy-tale ending, but there is a catch: *It was not easy.*

Both of them had to work the program. They put forth effort, risked rejection and embarrassment, experienced pain, stretched muscles they had never used, failed, and learned through the process.

And, as we say good-bye, I want to remind you that anything worthwhile in life, including dating, involves effort, risk, pain, and failure. How do you get a good career? Does it just fall out of the sky? Of course not. You work on yourself and improve your skills. It takes effort. How do you have a good marriage? Ask people who have them, and they will tell you the same. It takes work. How do you get in shape? Same answer.

So dating is no different. It takes effort. My hope is that as you go forward, you will remember not only that, but something else as well:

It is worth it.

No one will put forth effort if there is no payoff. In fact, that is why some people give up on dating altogether. The payoffs have been few. But my heartfelt belief is that if you do the things you read about in this book, the payoffs can be huge because dating is not just about dating. It is about personal and spiritual growth. And that is how I want you to embark on this program. You will not just find dates; you will grow as a person, and as a result of that, you will find dates.

Growing as a person is exactly what God desires for you. In Matthew 6, Jesus talks about our tendency to worry about the things of life. Certainly worrying about relationships is one of those things. We obsess about how to make them work, where to find them, and how to keep them going. It is a real problem, as God knows. But, as Jesus says, fixing our relationships, or fixing any other area of our lives is not the first step. The first step is always our spiritual growth, for *it is that growth that produces the very thing that we desire.* He puts it this way: "But seek first his kingdom and his righteousness, and all these things will be given to you as well" (Matt. 6:33).

As we seek God and his ways and as we grow in those ways, we will find more of what we are looking for as well. This is certainly true in dating. As you grow, your dating life changes. As you become healthier, you attract different kinds of people, and you become less attracted to those who are not good for you. As you grow healthier, you become more able to take the steps that will bring results in dating. As you grow, you avoid the patterns that have been keeping you stuck. As you grow, you find more of who you are, what you really want, and how to find it. And God directs your steps as you walk with him.

So, I leave you with two things: the *reality* that it is not easy, and the *encouragement* that it is worth it. I did not write a book that gives you some pie-in-the-sky garbage that makes dating sound as easy as some infomercial that promises you can lose weight while you sleep or eat cookies. I have shared with you what I believe is the truth. It will not happen without effort, but if you put out the effort, you will see results.

I want good dating for you. Ask God to help, ask him to show you what to do, and then get moving. My prayer is that you will find the dates worth keeping—and that you become one of those yourself.

God bless you!

Dr. Henry Cloud
Los Angeles

Boundaries in Dating
Making Dating Work

Dr. Henry Cloud &
Dr. John Townsend

Between singleness and marriage lies the journey of dating. Want to make your road as smooth as possible? Set and maintain healthy boundaries—boundaries that will help you grow in freedom, honesty, and self-control. If many of your dating experiences have been difficult, *Boundaries in Dating* could revolutionize the way you handle relationships. And even if you're doing well, the insights you'll gain from this much-needed book can help you fine-tune or even completely readjust important areas of your dating life. Written by the authors of the bestselling book *Boundaries*, *Boundaries in Dating* is your road map to the kind of enjoyable, rewarding dating that can take you from weekends alone to a lifetime with the soul mate you've longed for.

Softcover: 0-310-20034-2
Abridged Audio Pages® Cassette: 0-310-20155-0
Workbook: 0-310-23330-5
Curriculum: 0-310-23847-0

Pick up a copy today at your favorite bookstore!

ZONDERVAN™

GRAND RAPIDS, MICHIGAN 49530 USA

WWW.ZONDERVAN.COM

Boundaries

When to Say Yes, When to Say No to Take Control of Your Life

Dr. Henry Cloud &
Dr. John Townsend

Is your life out of control?
Do people take advantage of you?
Do you have trouble saying no?
Are you disappointed with God because of unanswered prayers?

Having clear boundaries is essential to a healthy, balanced lifestyle. A boundary is a personal property line that marks those things for which we are responsible. In other words, boundaries define who we are and who we are not.

Boundaries impact all areas of our lives:
- Physical boundaries
- Mental boundaries
- Emotional boundaries
- Spiritual boundaries

Often, Christians focus so much on being loving and unselfish that they forget their own limits and limitations. Dr. Henry Cloud and Dr. John Townsend offer biblically based answers to many tough questions, showing us how to set healthy boundaries with our parents, spouses, children, friends, coworkers, and even ourselves.

Hardcover 0-310-58590-2
Softcover 0-310-24745-4
Also available:
Abridged Audio Pages® Cassette 0-310-58598-8
Workbook 0-310-49481-8
Boundaries Groupware 0-310-22362-8
Boundaries Leader's Guide 0-310-22452-7
Boundaries Participant's Guide0-310-22453-5

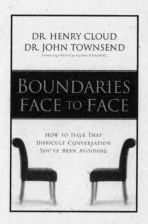

We want to hear from you. Please send your comments about this book to us in care of zreview@zondervan.com. Thank you.

GRAND RAPIDS, MICHIGAN 49530 USA

WWW.ZONDERVAN.COM